ESTONIA

LATVIA

THE BALTICS

LITHUANIA

THE BALTICS

BY JOHN F. GRABOWSKI

LUCENT BOOKS
P.O. BOX 289011
SAN DIEGO, CA 92198-9011

On Cover: Riga at night

Library of Congress Cataloging-in-Publication Data

Grabowski, John F.
    The Baltics / by John F. Grabowski.
        p. cm. — (Modern nations of the world)
Includes bibliographical references and index.
    ISBN 1-56006-734-9
    1. Baltic States—Juvenile literature. I. Title.   II. Series.
    DK502.35 .G7   2001
    947.9—dc21

00-012717

Copyright © 2001 by Lucent Books, Inc.
P.O. Box 289011, San Diego, CA 92198-9011
Printed in the U.S.A.

CONTENTS

FOREWORD

THE CURTAIN RISES

Through most of the last century, the world was widely perceived as divided into two realms separated by what British prime minister Winston Churchill once called the "iron curtain." This curtain was, of course, not really made of iron, but of ideas and values. Countries to the west of this symbolic curtain, including the United States, were democracies founded upon the economic principles of capitalism. To the east, in the Soviet Union, a new social and economic order known as communism prevailed. The United States and the Soviet Union were locked for much of the twentieth century in a struggle for military, economic, and political dominance around the world.

But the Soviet Union could not sustain its own weight, burdened as it was by a hugely inefficient centralized government bureaucracy, by long-term neglect of domestic needs in favor of spending untold billions on the military, and by the systematic repression of thought and expression among its citizens. For years the military and internal police apparatus had held together the Soviet Union's diverse peoples. But even these entities could not overcome the corruption, the inefficiency, and the inability of the Communist system to provide the basic necessities for the Soviet people.

The unrest that signaled the beginning of the end for the Soviet Union began in the satellite countries of Eastern Europe in 1988—in East Germany, followed by Hungary, and Poland. By 1990, the independence movement had moved closer to the Soviet heartland. Lithuania became the first Baltic nation to declare its independence. By December 1991, all fifteen union republics—Armenia, Azerbaijan, Belarus, Estonia, Georgia, Kazakhstan, Kyrgyzstan, Latvia, Lithuania, Moldova, Russia, Tajikistan, Turkmenistan, Ukraine, Uzbekistan—had done the same. The Soviet Union had officially ceased to exist.

Today the people of new nations such as Uzbekistan, Latvia, Belarus, Georgia, Ukraine, and Russia itself (still the largest nation on earth) must deal with the loss of the certainties of the Soviet era and face the new economic and social challenges of the present. The fact that many of these regions have little if any history of self-governance adds to the problem. For better or worse, many social problems were kept in check by a powerful government during the Soviet era, and long-standing cultural, ethnic, and other tensions are once again threatening to tear apart these new and fragile nations. Whether these regions make an effective transition to a market economy based on capitalism and resolve their internal economic crises by becoming vital and successful participants in world trade; whether their social crises push them back in the direction of dictatorship or civil war, or move them toward greater political, ethnic, and religious tolerance; and perhaps most important of all, whether average citizens can come to believe in their own ability to improve their lives and their own power to create a government and a nation of laws that works in their own best

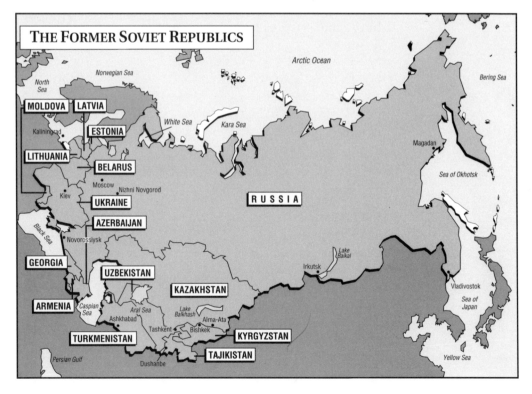

THE FORMER SOVIET REPUBLICS

interests, are questions that the entire world, not just former Soviet citizens are pondering.

Sociologists and political scientists alike point to instability in the former Soviet republics as a serious threat to world peace and the balance of global power, and therefore it is more important than ever to be accurately informed about this politically and economically critical part of the world. With Modern Nations: Former Soviet Republics, Lucent Books provides information about the people and recent history of the former Soviet republics, with an emphasis on those aspects of their culture, history, and current situation that seem most likely to play a role in the future course of each of these new nations emerging from the shadows of the now vanished iron curtain.

INTRODUCTION

SIMILAR BUT DISTINCT

The three Baltic nations of Estonia, Latvia, and Lithuania are tied together by geography and a shared history. Bordering the Baltic Sea, the nations have come under the rule of foreign powers for the better part of seven centuries, with only Lithuania enjoying a period of independence. At the start of the twentieth century, they were under the brutal thumb of Russia. Each country achieved autonomy briefly following World War I, but again fell under Soviet influence (as former British foreign secretary Douglas Hurd put it, "stolen or kidnapped from the European family"[1]). In 1991, the three nations reestablished their independence.

The peoples of the Baltic States share some of the same personality traits and interests. They have a strong love of nature and their surroundings. Anatol Lieven, author of *The Baltic Revolution*, wrote, "Love of nature, and most especially of forests and trees, are the keys to understanding and liking much of Baltic culture."[2] Perhaps because of their history, they tend to be suspicious of strangers. They are also tenacious and stubborn, with a strong sense of nationalism and a desire for independence. Nationhood for the inhabitants of the Baltics is sacred, simply because it has long been forbidden. The goal of independence has helped them endure centuries of dominance by neighboring countries, as one conqueror after another has tried, and failed, to break their spirit. This will to endure in the face of countless hardships is perhaps their defining characteristic.

Despite these common bonds, however, the countries consist of three very different peoples. Their languages and cultures are different, as are their national dispositions. In general, Estonians are very reserved ("An Estonian's motto for behavior," relates Estonian psychiatrist Anti Liiv, "is: May your face be as ice"[3]), Lithuanians are very emotional, and Latvians somewhere in the middle ("Latvians like to think of themselves as dreamers with a practical streak,"[4] wrote Anatol

Lieven). Perhaps because of the years spent under Moscow's iron grip, the peoples of the three nations are anxious to downplay their similarities and celebrate their differences.

Estonians speak a language related to Finnish, stemming from the Finno-Ugric group. They often compare themselves to their neighbors across the Baltic Sea, the Finns and Swedes. They are generally polite, but not as friendly as natives of the other Baltic countries. This is largely because of their dislike of the Russians, who swarmed across the border during the period of Russification over the last half of the twentieth century.

Lithuanian children participate in a 1989 independence rally. Like the other Baltic nations, Lithuania is struggling to establish its own identity since winning independence in 1991.

Latvians are more accepting of the Russians, in part because of the large number who have come to work in their industrial plants. Native Latvians make up just 54 percent of the nation's population. They are known for their kindness and ability to get along with others, a trait sometimes mistaken as a sign of weakness by those more aggressive in furthering Latvian goals.

The most self-confident people in the Baltic States can be found in Lithuania. Their self-assuredness is undoubtedly a vestige from the time when the country was a power in Eastern Europe. Their drive to succeed is seen by many as an attempt to regain what they view as their rightful place in the modern world.

These three distinct societies enter the new millennium facing the same formidable challenges and perceived threats. They must prevail in the face of economic, environmental, and ethnic instability, obstacles not of their own making. As they endeavor to establish their own identities in the modern world, their fates are intertwined yet again.

1

A LONG, EMBATTLED HISTORY

The geographic position of the Baltic States has ensured that for centuries they have found themselves controlled by various stronger groups and countries. The nations lie at the center of the European continent, accessible to the West by way of the Baltic Sea. Numerous rulers have desired this "window to the West" for its commercial advantages. As a result, the native Balts have been the subject of repression since the time when pagan tribes were the region's only inhabitants.

GEOGRAPHY AND CLIMATE

The word *Baltic* was first used in the eleventh century by the German chronicler Adamus Bremen. Writing in Latin, he referred to the *Mare Balticum*, or Baltic Sea. Some researchers believe that the name alluded to the shape of the sea itself. (The Danish word for belt is *bœlte*. The sea extends like a wide belt in a northeasterly direction from its westernmost point near Denmark.) Others theorize that it is derived from the Prussian word, *balt*, which means a landlocked bay. Still others insist it comes from the Lithuanian word *baltas*, or white, referring to the white-capped, windswept sea. Whatever the truth may be, the sea bordering the region has been a focal point in the history of the three nations of Estonia, Latvia, and Lithuania.

The republics of Estonia (*Eesti Vabariik*), Latvia (*Latvijas Republika*), and Lithuania (*Lietuvos Respublika*) lie along the eastern coast of the Baltic Sea in central Europe. The Baltic Sea is connected with the Caspian and Black Seas by the Volga-Baltic waterway and the Volga-Don Canal. Finland lies to the north, directly across the Gulf of Finland, while Sweden is located west across the sea.

Estonia is the smallest and northernmost of the three countries. *Eesti*—the country's name in Estonian—is probably derived from *Æstii*, which was the name given to all the tribes in the area by a Roman chronicler in 100 B.C. Scandinavians to the north referred to the land south of the Gulf of Finland as *Eistland*, and to the people as *aistr*. Eventually, the name came to be applied only to the Estonians.

Estonia is bordered by the Gulf of Finland on the north and Russia on the east. Lake Peipus, the largest lake in the region, and the Narva River form much of the eastern boundary. The Baltic Sea and Gulf of Riga lie to the west, as do more than one thousand islands that are Estonian territory. The four largest islands are Saaremaa, Hiiumaa, Muhu, and Vormsi.

To Estonia's south lies Latvia, the largest of the Baltic nations, approximately equal in area to the state of West Virginia. Prior to 1800, modern-day Latvia was known as either *Lettland*, *Leththia*, or *Lothwa*. *Let* or *lat* likely refer to the Leta or Lata Rivers that flow near the city of Vilnius in present-day Lithuania, where the Latvians lived before migrating north. The Livs, a tribe that settled among the Latvians, modified the name to *Latvis*, which means "forest clearers."

Russia is Latvia's neighbor to the east, and Belarus and Lithuania form its southern boundary. In the northwest, the Gulf of Riga forms a wide inlet that sweeps down into the country's midsection. Latvia is divided into five regions: Kurzeme, Zemgale, Vidzeme, Latgale, and Lielriga, the area around the capital city of Riga.

Lithuania, the third Baltic nation, is bordered by Belarus to the east and south, and Poland and the Russian enclave of Kaliningrad to the southwest. Its coastline on the Baltic to the west is the narrowest of the three countries. The derivation of the country's name is a matter of dispute. Some suggest that it may have come from the Lithuanian word *lietus*, which means rain (or land of rain). Others believe it evolved from the Latin word for tubes, *litus*. This may have referred to the wooden horns played by the natives of the area. Most researchers, however, believe the name was derived from the name of a river, although there is no evidence that a river with a similar name ever existed.

The region occupied by the Baltic republics, approximately equal in area to the state of Washington, is part of the great East European Plain, which extends across much of Europe up to the Ural Mountains. The plain rarely reaches heights of one thousand feet. The highest points in the nations are Suur Munamagi in Estonia (1,043 feet), Galzinkalns in Latvia (1,024 feet), and Juozapines/Kalnas in Lithuania (958 feet).

The region's flat lowlands and gently rolling hills are of glacial origin. They were formed millions of years ago during the Pleistocene Epoch. Large glaciers moved over the surface of the land, leaving deposits in the form of eskers (long, low ridges composed of glacial sand and gravel), moraines (rock debris transported by the moving ice), and drumlins (elongated hills of debris). The melting ice also resulted in hundreds of lakes dotting the terrain. Numerous rivers cross the area as well, emptying into the Baltic Sea, Gulf of Riga, or Gulf of Finland. The two main rivers are the Neman (*Nemunas*) and the Western Dvina (*Daugava*). The latter, sometimes referred to as the "mother of rivers," was an important ancient trade route linking the Baltic and Black Seas. Swamps and marshes are also common in the region, which is prone to flooding.

The coastal area is marked by pine forests, which are responsible for one of the region's defining products. Millions

of years ago, pine trees covered much of the area's marshland. When resin from the trees seeped out, it settled in the
silt and eventually hardened. This petrified resin, known as
amber, is washed up on the shorelines by the sea. (Around
1250 B.C., this area became known as "the land of amber.")
The white beaches of this "Amber Coast" have long been a
popular resort destination for Balts, Russians, and Poles.

The capitals of Estonia and Latvia—Tallinn and Riga, re-
spectively—are important Baltic ports. Vilnius, the capital of
Lithuania, however, lies considerably inland. Klaipeda is
Lithuania's only significant port.

Tallinn, which is one of the northernmost points in the
Baltics, lies at a latitude approximately equal to that of
southern Alaska. The climate of the Baltics is generally tem-
perate and humid as a result of the prevailing air masses that
sweep in from the Atlantic Ocean. The three nations have
cool summers and damp winters, with an average precipita-
tion ranging from twenty to thirty inches per year.

*For centuries
vacationers have
enjoyed the beaches
along the shoreline of
the Baltic Sea.*

AMBER

The Greek poet Homer was the first to call the Baltic shoreline
the Amber Coast. The brilliant, golden fragments that the
name refers to were the basis of the earliest trade in the region.

According to legend, amber are fragments of the underwater castle of the sea goddess Jurate. The truth is not quite so
romantic. Amber is actually the fossilized resin of prehistoric
pine trees that formed a layer beneath the surface of the
seabed. Chunks occasionally are scraped away and washed
ashore. The attraction of the solidified sap is what lies within.
The substance attracted gnats and other insects, who became
trapped by its sticky surface. These primeval, fossilized insects
can often be seen in the stones when they are held up to the
light.

Although amber is found throughout the world, the largest
deposits occur along the shores of the Baltic Sea. One of the
best places to learn about this prized stone, sometimes referred to as "Lithuanian gold," is at the Amber Museum of
Palanga, Lithuania, which houses a collection of approximately twenty-five thousand items.

*Fossilized insects trapped millions of years ago in pine-tree resin
can be seen in amber found along the Baltic coast.*

EARLY TRIBES

The first inhabitants of the region settled along the eastern Baltic shores several thousand years ago. In the north, Finno-Ugric tribes that were ancestors of the modern-day Estonians occupied the land all the way down to present-day Latvia. To the south lived the forefathers of the modern-day Latvians and Lithuanians, who originally came from central Russia. The majority of these tribes have become extinct over the years.

Toward the end of the first century, the Roman historian Tacitus spoke of the people who lived around the Baltic Sea. "Strangely beastlike and squalidly poor," he wrote, "neither arms [weapons] nor homes have they. Their food is herbs, their clothing skin, their bed the earth."[5] The Baltic and Roman cultures had been in contact with each other because of the extensive trade in amber that had developed, a trade that saw the stone find its way as far as ancient Egypt and Greece. The relationship continued until the fall of the Roman Empire.

In the middle of the seventh century, Viking raiders began sweeping down from Scandinavia. These raids were relatively peaceful, since the Vikings were mainly interested in trading routes. Their main objective was to reach the Muslim and Byzantine traders to the south. As a result, several settlements were established in the region, mostly on the south shore of the Baltic Sea. From here, the Vikings followed the Dnieper and Volga Rivers down through present-day Russia and Ukraine. The Balts were allowed to live their quiet existence and continue their pagan customs, which included worshiping the forces of nature. This period of relative peace would last for approximately six hundred years.

By the year 1000, Christianity had taken hold in western and southern Europe. In 1180, a missionary monk, Meinhard of Bremen, landed on the coast of what is today Latvia. Appointed as a bishop, he preached Christianity to the tribe known as the Livs, but without much success. The force of Christianity, however, was not to be denied.

THE TEUTONIC KNIGHTS

At the beginning of the thirteenth century, the pope sent German religious crusaders, known as the Knights of the Sword, to invade southern Estonia and Latvia and spread Christianity

Roman historian Tacitus described the ancient tribes of the Baltics as primitive and poor.

among the pagans who lived there. The invaders established a bishopric at Riga in 1201. Since the peasants had no centralized organization to govern them, they were no match for the crusading Germans from the south. The Knights of the Sword were eventually consolidated with other orders in 1237, becoming known collectively as the Teutonic Order. Within twenty-five years, most of Estonia and northern Latvia were under the control of the Order of Teutonic Knights. They called the country Livland, after the Livs who occupied the coastal area. In Latin, this translated into Livonia.

One area that was not under the control of the Teutonic Knights was the northernmost part of Estonia, near Tallinn. It had been invaded from the north in 1219 by the forces of King Waldemar II of Denmark. (The name of the Estonian capital, Tallinn, is Estonian for "Danish town.") By the middle of the fourteenth century, however, many of the natives had become dissatisfied with Danish rule. A series of revolts against the invaders, including the bloody St. George's Night Uprising of 1343, discouraged the Danes. Finally, in 1346, they surrendered their control of northern Estonia to the Germans.

The Germans established themselves as the dominant force in the area. They settled down as nobility and treated the natives as serfs (those bound to the land and owned by a lord). Since the natives were allowed to retain most of their customs, however, this period was generally one of peaceful coexistence.

Commerce was controlled by the German craftsmen and merchants who had followed the crusaders into the region. The larger cities became members of the Hanseatic League, an organization established by the merchants to protect the trading interests of its members. The success of trade in cities having access to the Baltic Sea was not lost on neighboring countries to the east.

This sculpture adorns the tomb of a grandmaster of the Order of Teutonic Knights, German crusaders who took control of most of the Baltics in the thirteenth century.

EARLY LITHUANIA

To the south of Livonia, much of the land was protected by thick forests and marshland. Because of this, the early Lithuanian tribes were able to avoid conquest by the Germans. Around 1230, as further protection against the threat of invaders, the tribes united under Grand Duke Ringaudas and his successor, Mindaugas. In 1236, they crushed the Livonian knights in the battle of Saule.

However, Mindaugas eventually accepted Christianity for political reasons. By doing so, he was able to be crowned king of Lithuania in 1253 under the authority of Pope Innocent IV. His conversion also gave the crusading Germans less reason to try to take over the region.

Mindaugas consolidated the Lithuanian lands into a powerful grand duchy (dukedom). Ten years later, however, he

THE HANSEATIC LEAGUE

From the thirteenth to the fifteenth century, northern European trading activity was dominated by the Hanseatic League. The league was an association (Hansa) of German-dominated Baltic trading cities that banded together to protect their common interests. Lubeck, Germany, was its main base of operations.

The league attempted to safeguard its members' ships from pirates on the Baltic and North Seas and encourage safe navigation by building lighthouses. It controlled trade throughout the region by generating commercial laws and founding trading bases. It also gained advantages for its members, such as exemptions from taxes and tolls paid by others. If its requests for these favors were denied, the league would enforce embargoes or blockades to halt trade. On rare occasions, these policies led to warfare.

At the height of its power, the league included approximately one hundred towns, and another hundred were members at some time or other. Tallinn, Riga, Visby, Danzig, and Wismar played leading roles during the organization's period of dominance.

The league's eventual decline was partly due to the increased strength of some of the neighboring nations, such as Russia, and the Lithuania-Poland alliance. In addition, the opening of new markets to the west diverted much of the rewas assassinated by his nobles, who were dissatisfied with his policies, and the country returned to paganism. Grand Duke Gediminas, one of Mindaugas's successors, founded the capital of Vilnius and expanded the Lithuanian state to the south and to the east. By the fourteenth century, it had become one of the largest empires in Europe, extending all the way from the Baltic Sea to the Black Sea.

Gediminas divided his empire among his seven sons. After a period of familial infighting, his grandson Jogaila came to power. Facing increased pressure from the Teutonic Knights, Jogaila realized the need for an ally. He joined forces with Poland, marrying twelve-year-old Queen Jadwiga in 1386 to become King Wladyslaw II. As part of the arrangement, Jogaila agreed that Lithuania would accept Catholicism, becoming the last European country to do so. With the

gion's trade. The Hanseatic League declined in importance through the 1500s, and its remaining nine members met for the last time in 1669.

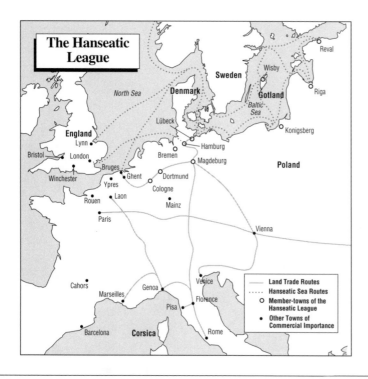

The Hanseatic League

marriage, Poland and Lithuania formed a loose confederation. Jogaila's cousin Vytautas was made grand duke of Lithuania and the Jogaila dynasty would rule over the Polish-Lithuanian kingdom until 1572.

Together with their Polish allies, the Lithuanians soundly defeated the Teutonic Knights at Tannenberg on July 15, 1410. German expansion to the east was halted. Under Vytautas the Great, the grand duchy extended its borders and became one of the largest—and most powerful—states in Europe. A new threat, however, loomed to the east.

THE LATE MIDDLE AGES

This nineteenth-century painting by Jan Matejko depicts the battle of Grunwald. Eastward expansion by Germany came to an end with the defeat of the Teutonic Knights by a Polish-Lithuanian army in 1410.

Poland and Lithuania maintained their loose alliance under a common ruler until 1569. On July 1 of that year, a parliamentary meeting transformed the union into a Commonwealth of Two Peoples under the Union of Lublin. Although each nation was administered separately and had its own armed forces, they elected a common sovereign and parliament. This union remained in effect until the latter part of the eighteenth century.

THE WEDDING OF PRINCESS JADWIGA

Since infancy, Princess Jadwiga of Poland had been betrothed to Wilhem von Habsburg. In 1385, plans were made for the couple to marry in Kraków, at the time, the capital of Poland. The festivities surrounding the wedding were already under way when a company of Lithuanian nobles arrived in the city for a meeting with the Polish aristocracy. As a result of the meeting, the wedding was called off. The Lithuanians had proposed that their grand prince, Jogaila, marry Jadwiga instead of Habsburg. This would allow the two states to join forces and resist the Teutonic Knights, who had invaded the Baltic region.

The union made sense from the points of view of both countries. Jadwiga, however, saw it differently. The eleven-year-old princess was appalled at the thought of marrying the much older Jogaila.

The marriage of convenience took place the next year, with Lithuania agreeing to convert to Catholicism as part of the arrangement. The union had its desired effect. The combined Polish-Lithuanian forces eventually defeated the Teutonic Knights at Tannenberg in 1410, effectively ending the Germans' advance.

Meanwhile, the Teutonic Knights, together with the merchants of the Hanseatic League, were continuing their domination of Livonia. By the middle of the sixteenth century, however, the trade opportunities with the West presented by the waterways in the Baltic region attracted the interest of the Russian czar, Ivan Vasilyevich, or as he became known, "Ivan the Terrible." His interest would ultimately have disastrous effects on the Baltics.

The Livonian War began with Ivan's attack in 1558. In the beginning, his forces enjoyed several successes, an important one being the seizure of the Estonian port of Narva. By 1561, the Livonian forces had been worn down and forced to disband. The Latvian territory was broken up into three parts: Estland, Livonia, and Courland. The Germans in the northern part of Estonia (Estland) looked to Sweden for protection. To the south (Livonia), the local nobles ceded their power to the Polish-Lithuanian Commonwealth for the same reason. An autonomous duchy (Courland) was formed from the provinces of Kurzeme and Zemgale to the west and south.

The Livonian War continued until Russia was forced out of Estonia by the Swedes in 1583. During the ensuing period, Poland and Sweden battled for Baltic supremacy. As a result of these conflicts, Sweden took over Riga in 1621 and Vidzeme in 1629 under the Truce of Altmark. The day that King Gustavus Adolph II (or Adolphus) marched into Riga is the beginning of what is referred to as the "good Swedish times," a period marked by cultural advancement. The rights of the German nobles were limited by the Swedes, and many nobles had their manors taken over by the state. The rights of the peasants, on the other hand, were expanded, and schools to educate them were established throughout the country. In Estonia, Tartu University opened in 1632.

RUSSIAN RULE

The Russians, however, had not given up. Peter the Great, who succeeded Ivan, began the Great Northern War with Charles XII of Sweden at the beginning of the eighteenth century. The conflict raged from 1700 to 1721. The cities of Riga and Tallinn fell to the advancing forces. The Russians emerged victorious and the Baltics lay in ruins. Russia had acquired the "window to the West" it had long desired. It had access to the Baltic Sea and, with it, trade with the West.

Sweden's claims to Vidzeme (central Latvia) were lost with the Treaty of Nystad, which ended the war. The weakened Polish-Lithuanian Commonwealth was eventually partitioned among Prussia, Russia, and Austria in three stages. Latgale (eastern Latvia) was annexed by the Russians in 1772. By 1795, Russia had control of nearly the entire Baltic region.

Peter did not impose Russian institutions on his new subjects. They were allowed to keep their own laws and religions. The German nobles had many of their rights and privileges restored, while the peasants resumed living under conditions as poor as ever.

When Alexander I became czar of Russia at the beginning of the nineteenth century, things began to change, particularly in Estonia, Livonia, and Courland. Serfdom, a form of

slavery that had been established under the Germans, was soon abolished, and the peasants were eventually given the right to purchase land. Since few had the resources to do so, however, most of the land remained in the hands of the German nobles until the end of the century. Many peasants took jobs as laborers for the same landowners who had been their masters.

A century of Swedish rule ended when Russian forces led by Peter the Great retook the Baltics in the Great Northern War, which began in 1700.

In time, the availability of peasant labor encouraged manufacturing in the region, and many of the former serfs relocated to the cities. The production of textiles became a major industry. The construction of a railway between Tallinn and St. Petersburg, completed in 1870, also provided many jobs. By the end of the century, Estonia had become one of the most industrialized regions of the entire Russian Empire.

THE NATIONAL AWAKENING

The latter part of the nineteenth century, which would become known as the National Awakening, was also an active time of scholarship and intellectual breakthrough in Estonia. Literacy spread, and underground periodicals appeared in the native language. (The czar had made the use of the Russian language mandatory, and publication of books in anything other than the Russian Cyrillic alphabet had been banned.) With more and more people able to read, books in the mother tongue came to be considered important symbols of national culture. The glorification of Estonian literacy led to a heightened consciousness of a national identity.

The year 1869 saw the earliest public expression of this Estonian national identity when the first song festival was held in Tartu. In Latvia, a group of students known as the *Jaunlatviesia* published the *St. Petersburg Paper* in a successful attempt to make the citizens more aware of their Latvian heritage. In 1873, Latvia hosted an all-Latvian song festival. These festivals would later become rallying points for national feelings.

These women musicians dressed in traditional clothes take part in a Latvian song festival.

In Lithuania, Russian social institutions played a much bigger role than they did in Estonia and Latvia. Many Lithuanians had joined their former commonwealth partners in ineffective uprisings against Russia in 1812, 1831, and 1863. As a result, the czarist regime in Russia came down especially hard on the natives, mounting a rigid campaign of Russification (a drive to impose all elements of Russian society on the natives and eradicate all traces of native customs and traditions). The University of Vilnius was closed, and the Lithuanian legal code abolished. Following the 1863 revolt, Count Muravyov, nicknamed "the Hangman," was sent to Lithuania to restore order. He did his best to see that most traces of ancient Lithuania were eliminated. Russian became the only language sanctioned for use in schools and other public areas. The Catholic Church had played an important role in Lithuania's state affairs. To counteract this, Russia promoted the spread of the Russian Orthodox Church. Only Orthodox subjects, for example, were allowed to buy property. Russian repression caused thousands of natives to emigrate to North America. It also, however, kindled a revival of interest in Lithuanian culture and tradition.

The nationalist movements in the Baltics took on greater fervor as the world entered the twentieth century. Illegal political parties began springing to life. In Estonia and Latvia, poverty-stricken peasants took to the countryside, burning and looting the manors of the German nobles. Discontent among the working class made the situation more and more unstable. In a general strike on January 24, 1905, nearly fifty thousand Latvian workers took to the streets in protest. In that country alone, more than six hundred people were killed, including nearly one hundred Germans. British historian Rowlinson Carter wrote, "It was a violent time in the Baltic states, where many delighted in torching the grand German manors and other buildings of the ruling class. It was the start of a savage century."[6] The Russians fought back, and several thousand Latvians were executed. Many prominent citizens were forced into exile, including Latvia's national poet, Janis Rainis.

The Russian Revolution of 1905 spurred further action by the nationalists. In the south, a congress of elected Lithuanian delegates demanded the establishment of an autonomous state, making Lithuania the first Russian province to make such a demand. The Russians refused. However, they did agree to several concessions, including the reintroduction of the Lithuanian language in schools. The nationalist movement increased in strength.

INDEPENDENCE ON THE HORIZON

World War I proved pivotal to the cause of Baltic independence. The conflict came about, in part, because of the aggressive policies of the great European powers and the unrest among many of the subject peoples. The opposing sides were the Allies (Britain, France, Russia, and Italy) and the Central Powers (Germany, Austria-Hungary, Bulgaria, and the Ottoman Empire). By the beginning of 1917, German troops in the fight against czarist Russia occupied all of Lithuania and most of Latvia, although the Russians still controlled Estonia and eastern Latvia. The Russian Revolution of 1917 changed matters considerably.

In February, following several losses to German troops, the czarist government was overthrown, and a provisional government established. The new regime allowed the Estonians to form an autonomous Estonian government. That July, an Estonian National Council (*Maapaev*) was elected, with Konstantin Päts appointed premier. Similarly, elections were held in the northern part of Latvia not occupied by the Germans. The Latvian National Political Conference requested complete autonomy in July. Despite still being occupied, Lithuania demanded similar autonomy from the Russian provisional government.

Later that year, the Bolsheviks, a Communist party (one that supports an economic system in which the government owns the means of producing goods) led by Lenin, staged a coup which put them in power in Russia. This Bolshevik revolution alienated the Baltic nationalists. Since the nationalists were in favor of forming their own independent states, they disagreed with the Communists, who wanted to retain control of the Baltic provinces. With Russia in chaos, Lithuania and Estonia declared their independence on February 16, 1918, and February 24, 1918, respectively.

The Communist regime eventually surrendered its claims on the Baltic States to the Germans with the signing of the Treaty of Brest-Litovsk (Poland) on March 3, 1918. The Germans arrested and imprisoned leaders of the nationalist movements, and retained control until the imperial German government collapsed with the Allies' victory in November. The Latvian People's Council declared Latvia independent on November 18, 1918, and set up a national government under the leadership of Karlis Ulmanis.

With the Germans' defeat, the Russians declared the Treaty of Brest-Litovsk null and void. Communist forces again entered Estonian and Latvian territory. The Russians remained a force until a counteroffensive was mounted against them in January 1919. Within weeks, Estonian forces

under Colonel Johan Laidoner forced the Russians to withdraw. German troops abandoned the region by the end of the year.

The signing of the Treaty of Brest-Litovsk transferred control of the Baltics from the Bolsheviks to Germany in 1918.

On February 2, 1920, the Soviet government officially recognized the Republic of Estonia under the terms of the Tartu Peace Treaty. It renounced its claims to the territory for all time. That July, Estonia's freely elected Constituent Assembly, with August Rei as president, passed a declaration of independence and adopted a new constitution. On August 11, a Latvian-Soviet peace treaty was signed, and Russia similarly renounced its claims to Latvia.

Lithuania's recently declared autonomy was complicated by the country's long-standing relationship with Poland. Many Poles felt the Baltic state was part of Poland, dating back to the Commonwealth of Two Peoples formed under the Union of Lublin in 1569. Others believed that, at the least, Vilnius should become part of the homeland. According to a 1910 Russian census, 97,800 Poles occupied the city, compared with 75,500 Jews and just 2,200 Lithuanians.

Upon the collapse of Germany, Lithuania, like Estonia and Latvia, faced invasion by Russian troops. The Soviet army took over Vilnius on January 5, 1919, putting a pro-Bolshevik regime in place. The provisional Lithuanian government was evacuated to Kaunas, where it organized the Lithuanian National Army. On April 20, 1919, the Communists were driven from Vilnius by the Polish army (Poland had just recently declared its independence). The army prevented the Lithuanians from regaining the city. Vilnius was formally annexed by Poland in 1922 and would remain under Polish control for the better part of two decades. Lithuania refused to acknowledge this status and continued to claim Vilnius and its environs as its own.

By this time, the war was over. Estonia, Latvia, and Lithuania were recognized by the West as independent nations. In 1921, the three countries became members of the League of Nations. Their newly established autonomy, however, would not last for long. Darker days were yet to come.

The Road to
Independence

2

Much of the Baltics had been left in ruins by the retreating Communist army at the end of World War I. The three newly formed governments faced monumental rebuilding jobs as they tried to forge foundations for the future. It should not be surprising that they were not up to the task, and eventually gave way to more dictatorial regimes.

After World War II, the Baltics again found themselves under Russian rule. The Soviets attempted to crush their spirit, but the native Balts persevered. They would endure yet another half-century of suppression before rising up to defy their oppressors. This would be their greatest triumph of all.

Between the Wars

Following their independence, the Baltic nations adopted new liberal-democratic constitutions, with most power vested in their parliaments. A single-house parliament called the Riigikogu was formed in Estonia, where the prime minister was the head of state. The legislatures in both Latvia (Saeima) and Lithuania (Seimas) elected presidents, Janis Cakste and Antanas Smetona, respectively. This period saw a multiplicity of political parties in the new nations.

The new governments, however, proved ineffective when it came to improving the struggling economies. Unemployment rose and agricultural prices fell, creating an overall feeling of discontent. Within the space of a few years, more authoritarian forms of government replaced the administrations in each of the three nations. In Estonia, Konstantin Päts declared a state of emergency, dissolved parliament, and restructured the government in 1934. An election in 1938 installed him as the republic's first president. In Latvia, Prime

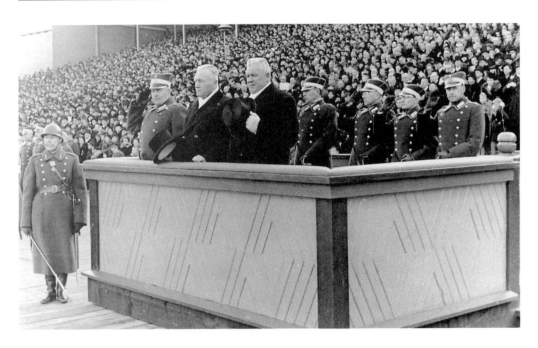

Prime Minister Karlis Ulmanis (front and center), shown here at an Independence Day parade, instituted authoritarian controls in his attempt to rebuild Latvia after World War I.

Minister Karlis Ulmanis also declared a state of emergency in 1934. The legislature and all political parties were dissolved. Like Päts, Ulmanis re-formed the government and ruled by decree, combining the offices of president and prime minister in 1936. In Lithuania, a takeover by the army in late 1926 put Smetona back in power. (He had been replaced by Aleksandras Stulginskis in 1920.) Smetona would remain as head of state until the Soviet occupation in 1940. The armed forces supported the regimes in the three nations. Opposition, not surprisingly, was limited. Occasional strikes by workers were put down with little resistance.

Because of the destruction caused by the war, economic reorganization was a top priority. Oil-shale fields in Estonia were opened, giving rise to a significant new industry. (Oil shale is a rock from which oil can be extracted through chemical methods. According to one legend, it was first discovered by a peasant who used it in the construction of a sauna. His horror at seeing the stone engulfed in flames can only be imagined.) The electronics industry developed in Latvia, but Lithuania remained primarily agricultural.

Faced with common problems and goals, Estonia and Latvia had formed an alliance in 1922. In 1934, Lithuania joined them, forming what became known as the Baltic Entente. The pact uniting them was intended to protect the countries from Nazi dreams of conquest, and to encourage cooperation in foreign, economic, and cultural affairs. The three nations tried to remain neutral in world affairs, despite the threats from Soviet Russia to the east and Nazi Germany to the west. Unfortunately, the two world powers had plans of their own.

WORLD WAR II

After the Estonians had driven the Bolsheviks back across the Russian border, Russia renounced its sovereignty over the country "voluntarily and for ever."[7] "Ever" turned out to be twenty years.

With World War II looming, foreign ministers Vyacheslav Molotov of the Soviet Union (which had been formed in 1922 under Russian leadership) and Joachim von Ribbentrop of Nazi Germany met on August 23, 1939, to sign the Nazi-Soviet Nonaggression Pact (also known as the Molotov-Ribbentrop Pact). Along with it, they signed a secret protocol. Under this protocol, which would not be acknowledged by the Soviets until fifty years later, the two powers divided Eastern Europe into two spheres of influence. This would enable them to pursue their own expansionist policies without having to worry about each other. Originally, Estonia and Latvia were earmarked for Russia, and Lithuania for Germany. Shortly thereafter, however, a revision to the original agreement placed most of Lithuania in the Soviet sphere, in exchange for additional territory and a sizable sum of gold.

After Germany invaded Poland, marking the start of World War II, the Soviets began to put their plan into effect. They forced the Baltic States to sign a Pact of Defense and Mutual Assistance that allowed the Communists to station military bases in their territory.

Within months, the Soviet Foreign Ministry accused the three Baltic nations of violating the pact. Using this as an excuse, Soviet ruler Joseph Stalin demanded that the existing governments in the three countries be replaced with ones that would be able to enforce the agreement. While most of the world's attention was focused on France's surrender to Germany, a new "people's government" was formed in Lithuania, followed by the establishment of similar administrations in Estonia and Latvia. The Communist Party came

Signing the Nazi-Soviet nonaggression pact in 1939, left to right are foreign ministers Joachim von Ribbentrop, Vyacheslav Molotov, and Soviet ruler Joseph Stalin.

to the forefront in the three nations, for the Soviets organized elections that put their candidates in office. This was not hard to do since they were the only ones allowed to run. The assemblies that were formed as a result voted for incorporation into the Soviet Union. When their requests were accepted in August 1940, the Soviet objective had been attained—the three Baltic nations were once again under Russian rule as Soviet Socialist republics.

The Soviets attempted to restructure life in the Baltics. Under a so-called land reform program, the government seized large estates and either turned them into state farms or distributed them in small parcels to individual farmers. Opposition to these new policies developed among the nationalist element, but anyone deemed a threat to Soviet rule was killed or deported. Many of those who were deported died in Siberia (in northeastern Russia) or Central Asia.

THE *ORZEL*

The Polish submarine *Orzel* (Eagle) was one of two such vessels ordered from Dutch shipyards by Poland in an effort to increase the strength of its navy. On September 8, 1939, the *Orzel* left the Gulf of Danzig for the open Baltic. It managed to avoid damage while traveling through a German minefield, but mechanical problems soon befell the ship, and its captain— Commander Henryk Kloczkowski—fell seriously ill. The *Orzel* headed for the Estonian port of Tallinn to undergo repairs and seek treatment for its commander.

The neutral Estonians were sympathetic to the plight of the Poles and began repairs on the sub. Under pressure from the Germans and Russians, however, they were instructed to arrest the crew and seize the ship. On September 18, the Estonians made a reluctant, halfhearted attempt to do so. When the Poles realized what was happening, they were able to overpower two guards, escape from the port, and vacate the area.

The escape would have serious consequences for Estonia. Moscow pointed to the incident as evidence that Estonia could not patrol its own shoreline. It used this as an excuse for invading the country, citing it as proof that Estonia had failed to protect its neutrality.

The *Orzel* eventually returned to action. On April 8, it became the first Polish warship to make a successful torpedo attack, as it sent the German transport *Rio de Janeiro* to the bottom of the sea. Sometime between May 23 and June 8, 1940, the *Orzel* apparently hit a mine and was lost in the North Sea. Its wreckage has never been found.

A BRIEF INTERRUPTION

The agreement between the Nazis and Soviets dissolved on June 22, 1941, when Adolf Hitler's German forces attacked the USSR. The Nazi occupation gave the Baltic nations hope that they would be allowed to reestablish their independence. Such was not to be the case, however. As Georg von Rauch wrote,

Many people in the Baltics mistakenly believed that occupation during World War II by the Germans, shown here landing in Lithuania, would reopen the door to national sovereignty.

> German troops were greeted as liberators by the vast majority of the indigenous population, and in all three territories there were popular risings against the Soviet army of occupation. Blissfully ignorant of Hitler's imperialist ambitions, surviving Baltic politicians were convinced that independence would soon be restored. . . . Later they were completely disillusioned by Hitler's refusal to allow them even a vestige of freedom.[8]

The German plan was to incorporate the three countries—and Belorussia (modern-day Belarus)—into the Reich, or Nazi empire. This new territorial unit was called Ostland.

The Germans set up local governments whose main purpose was to aid the war effort. To this end, a compulsory draft was declared, a move that was illegal in accordance with international law. The result was an increase in anti-German sentiment across the region. Underground nationalist bodies—the Central Council of Latvia, the Supreme Committee for the Liberation of Lithuania, and the National Committee of the Estonian Republic—were formed. These organizations could do nothing, however, to stem the Nazi reign of terror.

The Baltics suffered devastating losses during the war, among the highest in all of Europe. Gestapo (secret state police) units organized the liquidation of hundreds of thousands of Jews as part of Hitler's "final solution." The total number of deaths in the three countries was estimated at 250,000 in Lithuania, 180,000 in Latvia, and 90,000 in Estonia.

By 1944, German forces had experienced heavy losses in the fighting. Estonians declared the Republic of Estonia once again on September 18. The Russians, however, marched into Tallinn four days later. By the summer of the next year, all three Baltic nations had reverted to Soviet control.

SOVIET REPUBLICS

Following the war, the Russians continued their plan to integrate the three nations into the Soviet system, and to remove any reminders of Baltic independence. Secret police terrorized the populace. Nationalist groups were targeted, and members of the opposition were deported and killed in staggering numbers. Estimates of the number of deaths and deportations in the three countries approached the number of casualties suffered during the course of the war. Thousands of people escaped to the United States, Britain, Canada, Sweden, and Australia to avoid Russian rule. Tens of thousands of remaining nationalists withdrew into the Baltic forests to continue to resist the Soviets. These partisans, called the Forest Brothers, would continue their fight for the next decade, with some remaining in the woodlands for several years more. The resistance, however, proved futile.

The Soviets established economic policies of nationalization (converting businesses from private to government ownership and control) and collectivization (ownership and control of businesses by the people as a group). Estonia, Latvia, and Lithuania became highly urbanized, more so than any other republics in the Soviet Union. Branches of Soviet factories were formed in the three nations. Since these factories received raw material from—and delivered finished products to—other parts of the USSR, the Baltics became bound to the rest of the country economically. The industrialization in the three nations raised the standard of living above that in other parts of the Soviet Union.

The increased industrialization required that many workers come to the large cities. Russia sent thousands of immigrants to fill the new jobs. The immediate result of this surge of immigration was a decline in the percentage of natives in the three countries, particularly in Estonia and Latvia. By the mid-1980s, Latvia consisted of 54 percent Latvians, and Estonia 60 percent Estonians. In some border areas, such as

THE HILL OF CROSSES

Six miles north of the ancient town of Siaulia stands Jurgaiciai mound, perhaps the most reverential pilgrimage site in the entire Baltic region. Better known as the Hill of Crosses, it is a double-humped hillock covered with more than fifty thousand wood, iron, and stone crosses of every imaginable size and variety.

The crosses first began to appear in 1831 when natives began to place them to honor Lithuanians killed or deported in an anti-Russian revolt. More were added following a peasant rebellion thirty-two years later. By the end of the nineteenth century, the site had become a religious shrine.

Following World War II, the Soviet government declared the area "forbidden" and began to destroy the crosses. Many Lithuanians were exiled to Siberia during this period. When they began returning to their homes in 1956, the crosses again started appearing. The Hill of Crosses came to symbolize resistance to violence, oppression, and genocide. Once again, the Soviets attempted to raze the site. They bulldozed the area three times from 1961 to 1975. All attempts proved futile, however, for the crosses always reappeared.

The Hill of Crosses has become a sacred spot, and a monument to the spirit and courage of the Lithuanian people. In 1993,

Narva, where a division of the Soviet military-industrial complex was being developed, the percentage of Russians in the population surpassed 90 percent.

As the makeup of the populations changed, the countries became more Russified and the native cultures minimized. Religion was brutally suppressed. The Russian language was taught in schools, and students were indoctrinated into the perplexities of Soviet culture. The Russians saw no need to learn the local languages, thereby creating a feeling of separation from the natives. To many people around the world, Estonia, Latvia, and Lithuania, for all intents and purposes, no longer existed. They had lost their individuality and were now nothing more than states of the Soviet Empire. The Baltic national identities, however, never died. Anti-Russian feelings became stronger and stronger among the general populace.

one of the most extraordinary events of all occurred when Pope John Paul II celebrated Mass at the site.

The Hill of Crosses memorial in Lithuania has become a symbol of steadfast resistance to oppression.

Many of the Russian immigrants were white-collar workers who held important administrative positions in the government. The ruling Communist Party was heavily immigrant, and few natives of Estonia, Latvia, or Lithuania held positions of leadership. This balance of power changed slightly after Joseph Stalin died in 1953. A degree of local autonomy appeared under the more liberal policies of Premier Nikita Khrushchev. This became known as the "period of thaw." There were some attempts at economic reform, and repression was diminished. Many of those exiled to Siberia returned home.

By this time, many young nationalists had begun gravitating to the Communist Party, seeing it as a way of furthering their careers. Others believed they could help preserve their culture and language by joining the ranks of the ruling group. In 1957, a group of these national Communists in Latvia, led by the deputy premier of the Latvian Council of Ministers, Eduards Berklavs, began passing regulations with those goals in

Soviet repression in the Baltics initially decreased under Nikita Khrushchev, pictured here in front of the Soviet hammer and sickle symbol.

mind. They restricted immigration, tried to insist that government officials learn the Latvian language, and funded projects aimed at improving schools, hospitals, and housing. These programs were not looked upon favorably in the Russian capital of Moscow. Approximately two thousand of the national communists were removed from their positions in 1959, and Berklavs was exiled (only to return later as one of the leaders of the Latvian underground opposition). He was replaced with a pro-Moscow leadership that promoted Russification programs more strongly than ever. The trend toward openness suffered another setback when the Soviet Union crushed a similar reform movement in Czechoslovakia in 1968.

In Lithuania, the underground resistance centered around efforts to defend the Roman Catholic Church. In 1972, an underground periodical, *The Chronicle of the Lithuanian Catholic Church*, began to circulate among the nationalists. That same year, a nineteen-year-old student named Romas Kalanta made the ultimate protest against Soviet rule: He burned himself to death in a public park in Kaunas. This act launched a rebellion among students, some of whom copied Kalanta's act. The rebellion was put down when the army was sent in to intervene.

Estonian intellectuals spoke out against the use of force in suppressing protesters. Forty of them made their feelings known in a "Letter of the Forty" sent to the Communist newspapers *Pravda, Rahva Haa,* and *Sovetskaja Estonija.* They also voiced fears about the increased threat to the language and culture of the country. Nationalist feelings had risen to an all-time high. They would continue to escalate through the 1970s and '80s, when a change in Soviet leadership would set in motion a dramatic series of events.

INDEPENDENT ONCE AGAIN

Mikhail Gorbachev's ascension to power in Russia in 1985 brought many modifications to the Soviet system. He instituted a policy of glasnost (openness, or accessibility of information to the public) and attempted to revitalize the economy, the Communist Party, and society through a number of governmental and economic reforms known collectively as perestroika. Instead, however, he set into motion forces that eventually led to the Soviet Union's disintegration.

THE FOREST BROTHERS

When the Soviets implemented their policy of Russification following World War II, more than 100,000 Balts fled to the vast, wooded countryside to hide. Some were trying to save themselves from the secret police who sought to deport them. Others organized to resist the new Communist regime. These nationalists, who included everyone from farmhands to professors, became known as the Forest Brothers. The Brothers hoped that their extended resistance would encourage other democratic nations to intervene on behalf of Baltic independence.

In Lithuania, where the resistance was best organized, the armed guerrillas were able to control whole sections of the countryside until as late as 1949. Many of the Communist troops had second thoughts about venturing into the thick forests in an attempt to capture armed, angry gangs who had nothing left to lose. The nationalists wrecked power lines and ambushed Soviet patrols, generally making a nuisance of themselves.

By 1950, Soviet forces had gained the upper hand. Eventually, more than fifty thousand lives were lost in a battle that lasted well over a decade. Some individuals, however, managed to resist even longer, stubbornly refusing to submit to the Soviets.

In 1978, the last Forest Brother was hunted down near a river in Estonia. August Sabe was found by two KGB agents posing as fishermen. As they tried to arrest him, he managed to wrestle one into the river. With other agents on the way, however, Sabe knew there was no escape. He dove underwater and hooked himself to a submerged log. In a final act of defiance, he died rather than surrender to the Russians.

As the central power structure of the USSR weakened, a call for increased autonomy—and eventual independence—came from the member republics of the nation. In the Baltics, this mood was especially intense since the great majority of the population had never accepted their countries' incorporation into the Soviet Union. The three republics began to move, almost as one, to break free from Communist control.

A new national awakening began in 1987 with the first public demonstrations against the Soviets in nearly forty years. Environmentalists spoke out against the destruction caused by Soviet industry. Groups protested plans for the development of a new hydroelectric dam in Latvia and the construction of a mammoth phosphorite mine in Estonia. (Phosphorite is a rock that contains phosphate, which can be made into agricultural fertilizers.) In Estonia and Lithuania, nationalist groups memorialized the signing of the Molotov-Ribbentrop Pact that had consigned the countries to the Soviet sphere of influence. Latvians carried out ceremonies at Riga's Freedom Monument commemorating the Stalinist deportations of the 1940s. From these relatively small initial gatherings, the movement toward freedom began to snowball.

The Popular Front of Estonia, the Popular Front of Latvia, and the Lithuanian Reconstruction Movement, simply known as *Sajudis*, or "Movement," emerged in 1988 as vehicles for change. The *Sajudis* was established by some five hundred members of the intellectual class. The group supported democracy and independence, using mass meetings to advance its goals among the populace.

That summer, more than 100,000 people attended the Tallinn Song Festival. The event marked what became known as the Singing Revolution, since its demonstrations were peaceful and usually accompanied by the singing of previously banned national songs. Thousands of Estonians, meanwhile, heard Trivimi Velliste, minister of foreign affairs of the Republic of Estonia, make the first public call for Estonian independence. Later that year, the Estonian national legislature, guided by native son Vaino Valjas, passed amendments to the constitution that granted ultimate legal authority to the republic, rather than Moscow. It was a move considered the beginning of the end of the Soviet Union. Latvia and Lithuania followed in short order.

In 1989, Baltic representatives addressed the illegality of the Baltics' incorporation into the USSR before the Congress of People's Deputies in Moscow, the first national legislature chosen in openly contested elections since 1917. In response, the Soviet government proposed a policy that would grant increased autonomy to the fifteen republics of the USSR. "Recent events," read the proposal, showed "a need for radical transformations in the Soviet federation."[9]

A public call for independence in 1988 by Trivimi Velliste of Estonia was a turning point in the nationalist movement.

Later that year, a Baltic council commissioned to study the Molotov-Ribbentrop Pact concluded that the secret protocols awarding the three nations to the Soviet Union did, in fact, exist. In effect, this proved that Estonia, Latvia, and Lithuania had not been willing participants in becoming part of the Soviet Empire. Their "request" for admission into the Soviet Union in 1940 was nothing more than a sham.

Armed with this information, an estimated 2 million people from the three republics formed a human chain some four hundred miles long that crossed the land—from Tallinn through Riga to Vilnius—to express their feelings of unity. The date, August 23, marked the fiftieth anniversary of the pact. It was the largest and most dramatic anti-Soviet demonstration ever.

By 1990, the calls for increased autonomy had become demands for total independence. "We know there is no going back," said historian and future Estonian prime minister Mart Laar. "If we go back, the trains for Siberia will be very long."[10] Pro-independence candidates came to power in all three nations early in the year. On March 11, Lithuania's parliament declared its independence. Moscow attempted to undermine this action by setting up an economic blockade on April 17.

In the months that followed, Soviet forces occupied key buildings in Vilnius. They attacked the television tower, a key communications facility, on January 13, 1991, but demonstrators fought back. Fourteen Lithuanians died and hundreds were wounded, but the nationalists refused to back down. The killings were a defining moment for the Lithuanians, who realized they had reached a point where they could not turn back. As a correspondent in Lithuania for the *Christian Science Monitor* wrote, "Ultimately, Vilnius may have been the spark that lit the fuse that imploded the whole Soviet Union."[11]

Shortly after the massacre in Lithuania, another attempted seizure of a building, this time in Riga, resulted in more bloodshed. Five people were killed and ten injured in the Latvian capital as units of the Soviet Ministry of Internal Affairs Special Forces Detachment (the "Black Berets") attacked the Latvian Ministry of Interior. Tensions built to a fever pitch. The world watched breathlessly, wondering if the push for independence would be stifled once more. The European Union warned that it might cut off money promised to the USSR for food, economic aid, and technical assistance if the violence continued. Pressure from the world community mounted. Faced with this increased opposition, the Soviets backed down. No one, however, expected the shocking development to come.

AN ABORTED TAKEOVER

On August 18, 1991, Gorbachev was on vacation at a Black Sea resort. In several days, he was to sign an agreement giving greater autonomy to the republics of the Soviet Union.

The independence movement in Latvia stood its ground against Soviet military might in 1991.

While at the retreat, he was visited by a group of hard-line Communist Party leaders who feared that the move would be another step leading to the destruction of the Soviet Union. They demanded that he leave office. When he refused, they placed him under house arrest. They then announced that Vice President Gennadi Yanayev would be assuming presidential powers. With this return to the old regime looming over them, Latvia and Estonia declared independence outright.

The anti-Gorbachev contingent was thwarted when newly elected Russian president Boris Yeltsin was able to rally the reformist forces. Faced with this unexpected resistance, the plotters hesitated, and their intended overthrow of the government folded within four days. The failed takeover attempt led to the downfall of the Communist Party in the Soviet Union's central government.

With Moscow's authority on the brink of collapse, the Baltics had the opportunity they had long sought. One nation after another began to recognize Estonia's, Latvia's, and Lithuania's sovereignty. Within weeks, even the Soviet government was forced to do so. On September 17, the United Nations accepted the Baltic States. The long-awaited goal of Baltic independence was a reality at last.

By the end of December, all the Soviet republics except Georgia had proclaimed their independence. On December 8, 1991, the republics declared the end of the Soviet Union. The former republics were invited to join the Commonwealth of Independent States (CIS), a loosely structured confederation of the former Soviet republics that preserved the union in name only. Estonia, Latvia, and Lithuania politely declined. After years of Soviet repression, the Baltic States were ready to face the world on their own terms.

3

An Intermingling of Cultures

Many of the 7.6 million or so people who occupy the Baltic republics are descended from tribes that inhabited the region hundreds of years ago. Ancestors of some of the others are peoples who tried to subjugate those tribes. Still others emigrated from Russia over the last half of the twentieth century.

Despite their ethnic differences, many of their concerns are the same: how to provide food and shelter for their families, how to educate their children, how to live harmoniously with their neighbors, and how to survive in today's world. Since their independence, some aspects of life in the Baltics have experienced rapid change, while others have remained essentially the same as always. Although some (particularly the elderly) miss the security that came with Soviet rule, the majority enjoy the freedom to make their own choices.

Population

Changes in population size and ethnic makeup have followed similar patterns in the three Baltic nations. War losses and deportations were responsible for a decline in the populations in the 1940s, while Russian immigration accounted for significant increases following the war. Since independence, populations have generally declined. One reason for this is a negative natural growth rate (more deaths per thousand population than births). While the birth rate in each of the three nations is well below half the world average, the death rate is higher than the world rate. This is partially due to an inadequacy of medical services and supplies. In addition, many families have put off having children in times of economic uncertainty. Another factor has been the immigration of many non-Balts to their native lands. With stricter laws now limiting immigration into the three countries, the percentage of ethnic Balts will likely increase in the future.

The effects of Russian immigration during the Soviet period can be seen in the composition of the three populations. Lithuania is the most populous of the Baltic republics, with approximately 3,704,000 inhabitants. Ethnic Lithuanians make up 81.6 percent of the population. Russians are the second largest ethnic group (8.2 percent), followed by Poles (6.9 percent, mostly in Vilnius), Belarusians (1.5 percent), and Ukrainians (1 percent).

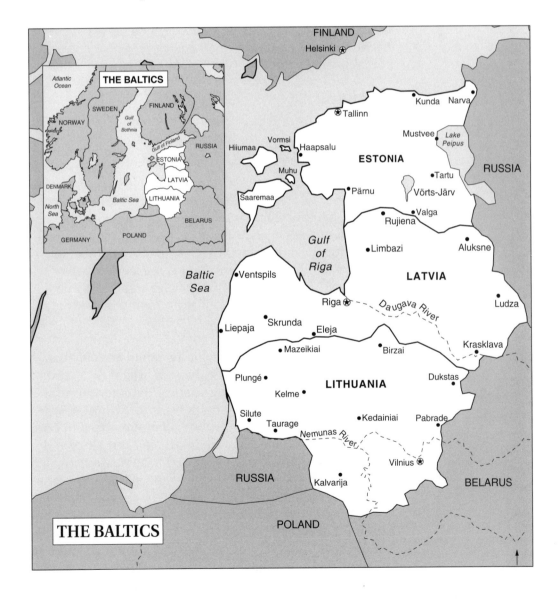

In Latvia, just 55.1 percent of the 2,445,000 inhabitants are ethnic Latvians. Russians account for another 32.6 percent of the population, including a large majority in the larger cities and towns. Belarusians make up 4 percent, followed by Ukrainians (2.9 percent), Poles (2.2 percent), and Lithuanians (1.3 percent).

Estonia is the least populous of the three nations, with just 1,447,000 inhabitants. Ethnic Estonians outnumber Russians by more than two to one (63.9 percent to 29 percent). Ukrainians have the next largest percentage (2.7 percent), then Belarusians (1.6 percent), and Finns (1 percent). As in Latvia, native Estonians tend to live in rural areas, with the Russians congregating in the cities where industrial jobs are found.

LANGUAGES

As the composition of the Baltic population has changed, so too has its attitude toward the spoken word. British journalist Edward Lucas once wrote,

> Language is of unique importance in the Baltics. Nowhere else in the world would one find three such small neighboring countries without an acceptable common language. Russian is almost universally spoken, but patriotic Estonians, Latvians, and Lithuanians feel as comfortable speaking the [former] occupier's language with each other as the Poles and Danes might have felt in 1946 if they could have communicated only in German.[12]

Today, that level of comfort has lessened even further.

Under Soviet occupation, Russian was a compulsory part of schooling. Nowadays, many Balts ignore it as a matter of national pride. This is especially noticeable in Latvia, where many schools that offered courses in both Latvian and Russian have been phased out since independence was achieved in 1991. These schools, which were introduced in the 1960s, offered each group classes in its own language. The original hope was that the schools would foster friendship and understanding between the two cultures.

English is spoken by an increasingly larger segment of the population. Eventually, it will likely become the second most-commonly spoken language, since it is the language spoken by most tourists and business visitors to the country. Ukrainian, Belarusian, Polish, and Finnish can also be heard in various regions, particularly in the larger cities where the majority of immigrants have chosen to settle.

Each of the three Baltic republics has its own official language. Those of Latvia and Lithuania are the last survivors of the Baltic family of Indo-European languages. Latvian and Lithuanian are remotely related to the Slavic tongues of Russia, Poland, and Ukraine. Citizens of the two Baltic countries can generally understand each other, but have trouble engaging in conversations of any depth.

Estonian is derived from the Finno-Ugric group. It is closely related to Finnish and, more distantly, to Hungarian. It is one of the more difficult European languages to learn, and has many different dialects. Estonian has been the official language of the land since 1919.

STANDARD OF LIVING

The change in attitude toward the Russian language is just one of the aspects of everyday life affected by the return to independence. Life after Soviet rule has certainly seen a change for the better in Estonia, Latvia, and Lithuania. There has been a significant rise in living standards, particularly when compared with other nations of the former Soviet Empire. However, they still remain below those in most of Europe. Members of the older generation sometimes yearn for the secure and more predictable life under the Communists. Most people, however, are appreciative of the changes that have taken place.

Although life may be as tough as it was in the past in many ways, it certainly is less tedious. With property now in the hands of private citizens, opportunities for the individual are greater. Who a person knows is far less important than how hard he or she is willing to work. For the first time in history, things formerly considered luxuries—such as cars and homes—are within the reach of many in the population.

However, much work remains to be done to correct the mismanagement of the Soviet era. Many basic facilities are not yet universal. Roads, utilities, housing, health care, and other necessities have far to go to match the level found in Western nations. Crime and drugs, meanwhile, have increased significantly. Undermanned police forces, low on

*Estonian families enjoy
a better standard of
living today than they
did under Soviet rule.*

resources, find themselves overwhelmed by muggings, vandalism, thefts, and burglaries. Organized crime has also begun to make inroads in the Baltics. Dealing with these problems is a necessity when accepting the responsibilities for deciding your own destiny. Most Balts would have it no other way.

THE ECONOMY

The improved standard of living in the Baltic nations is largely a result of an improved, diversified economy. The manufacturing sector employs about one-fourth of the workers in Estonia, one-fifth of those in Lithuania, and less than one-fifth of those in Latvia. A large proportion of these are Russian immigrants who came to the region during the period of Russification. The major commodities that are produced include construction materials, agricultural machinery, chemicals, processed foods, textiles, electronic goods, and wood products.

Latvia leads the three nations in the number of workers employed in agriculture. Dairy and meat products, potatoes, sugar beets, and various grains all come from Baltic farms. Since all three nations border the Baltic Sea, fishing also plays an important role in their economies. Service industries, such as wholesale and retail trade, transportation, communication, education, health, and social work, account for half of the workforce in the Baltics.

In economic matters, Estonians have perhaps benefited the most in the post-Soviet era, with Latvia ranking second, and Lithuania bringing up the rear. Approximately two-thirds of the combined gross national products of Estonia and Latvia come from industry, and about 20 percent from agriculture. Lithuania's figures are about 60 percent and 25 percent, respectively.

An important factor in Estonia's economic ascendancy has been its success in attracting foreign aid and investors. Latvia has had a troublesome time doing so, in part because of the collapse of Baltija Bank, the nation's largest commercial bank, in 1995. With their confidence shaken, foreign investors have been slow to pour money into the country. In Lithuania, unlike the other two Baltic States, foreigners are not allowed to own land and buildings. Consequently, it has had the greatest problem of all in attracting foreign investments.

RELIGION

Soviet rule affected not only the secular side of life in the Baltics but the spiritual side as well. The early Balts were pagans who worshiped the forces of nature. They did not become fully exposed to Christianity until the beginning of the thirteenth century when the German crusaders invaded what is now Estonia and Latvia. Lithuania did not convert to

Alexander Nevsky Cathedral, Tallin, Estonia. Religion was a unifying force in the Baltics during the difficult years of Communist oppression.

Christianity until nearly two hundred years later. Churches from these early years can be seen throughout the region. Occasional pagan worshipers can be found in parts of Lithuania. Many belong to the *Romuva* movement, which is attempting to resurrect the country's spiritual and folklore traditions from centuries gone by.

When the Protestant Reformation took place in the early sixteenth century, Tallinn and Riga became important religious centers. The Lutheran Church, however, mainly served the interests of the nobles and wealthy merchants. A large number of Catholics relocated to the Polish and Lithuanian territories. Many Old Believers (a sect of the Russian Orthodox Church that had been persecuted for its beliefs) also moved there following a split in the Russian church in the seventeenth century. The world's largest congregation of Old Believers can be found in Riga.

Other Protestant sects appeared in the Baltics toward the end of the nineteenth century. Jewish populations also developed, particularly in Vilnius, the "Jerusalem" of Lithuania. With the Nazi occupation during World War II, however, almost the entire Jewish population was either killed or deported.

When the Baltics fell under Soviet rule, many churches were converted to other uses. Priests and other clergy were imprisoned in an effort to discourage followers. The people, however, proved to be steadfast in their beliefs, as demonstrated by the recurring appearance of crosses on the Hill of Crosses in Lithuania.

Independence has given the Baltic people renewed hope. Lithuania has remained the most religious of the three countries, with Vilnius having reestablished itself as one of the leading centers of Catholicism in Europe. Almost 73 percent of the population is Roman Catholic. A strong religious belief has helped the people through the difficult Communist era. As a priest in one of the small towns explained, "When the Bolsheviks were in power, religion was the cement that held us together. They repressed us, they jailed us, harassed, yelled, and scolded us, all these things. But we held it together here."[13]

In Estonia, the Estonian Evangelical Lutheran Church is the state church, having been established in 1686. Orthodox Christianity is the nation's second largest religion. Since independence, divisions have surfaced among the Orthodox faithful, with many pushing for a break from the Moscow Patriarchate. In 1996, the Estonian Orthodox Church left Moscow's jurisdiction and renewed its ties with the Ecumenical Patriarchate of Constantinople, with whom it had total allegiance prior to Soviet rule.

The Jewish enclave in the Lithuanian city of Vilnius was decimated when the Nazis occupied the Baltics.

Lutheranism has also predominated in Latvia. There, the effects of Soviet domination were even more evident. As late as 1956, membership in the church had been greater than 600,000. Three decades later, the number had fallen to approximately 25,000. Many had fled the country in order to avoid Russian repression. A revival began in 1987, led by a core of young, rebellious, well-educated clergy. Demolished churches were rebuilt, and Sunday schools opened. Religion became fashionable, symbolizing rebellion against the government's authority.

Despite this resurgence, approximately 60 percent of the population in Estonia and Latvia does not have any religious affiliation. For many, solving the problems of everyday life has taken precedence over the spiritual side of existence. One of these problems is the matter of educating the young.

EDUCATION

A high priority is placed on education in the Baltics. Independence has brought with it a process of educational reform and restructuring of curricula that has produced impressive results. Each of the three nations in this highly educated society has a literacy rate of almost 100 percent.

In Estonia, the number of students in Estonian-language schools is about twice the number in Russian-language schools. The former offer twelve years of education—nine elementary and three secondary—while the latter offer eleven. By law, students must attend school up to the ninth grade. There are seventy-seven vocational schools in the nation and six universities. The oldest and largest university, with an enrollment of about seventy-six hundred, is Tartu University, founded by King Adolphus of Sweden in 1632. The others are Tallinn Technical University, Tallinn Pedagogical University, the Estonian Agricultural University, Tallinn Art University, and the Estonian Academy of Music. A four-year course of study system was adapted in the early 1990s, with baccalaureate, master's, and doctoral degrees awarded.

Latvian schools fall into three categories: those offering courses instructed in Latvian, those offering courses in Russian, and those offering courses in both languages. Nine years of primary schooling is compulsory. This may be followed by either three years in a secondary school or one to six years in a technical, vocational, or art school. Schools for other ethnic groups can also be found, catering to Poles, Estonians, Lithuanians, and Jews. Most institutions of higher learning are located in the capital city of Riga. These include the Riga Technical University and the University of Latvia. The location of these schools presents a problem to ethnic Latvians, who are more rural than the rest of the population. Because of this, the percentage of Latvians who complete some form of higher education is lower than the percentage for the population as a whole.

Lithuanians receive a free, compulsory education from the ages of six to sixteen. The system of education, developed in the period between World War I and World War II, has been revised since independence. In addition to Lithuanian, separate schools give courses of instruction in either the Russian or Polish language. At the university and vocational school level, the country has higher attendance than either of the other two Baltic republics. Vilnius University, Vytautas Magnus University, and Vilnius Technical University are three of the best-known institutions of higher learning.

This sixteenth-century illustration depicts Lithuania's Vilnius University, which is still a respected institution of higher learning.

One of the main changes in the restructuring of curricula that followed independence was the dropping of many Soviet ideological subjects, such as "scientific communism." The idea of a "Soviet school" philosophy has been replaced by one of a "national school." In addition, more schools and programs aimed at other ethnic groups have been established. This has been particularly noteworthy in Latvia, where many such schools were closed under the Soviet regime.

Food

Unlike education, some aspects of life in the Baltics have seen little change since the years of Soviet rule. Cuisine, for example, has remained basically the same for decades.

Baltic cooking does not rank among the great cuisines of the world. The food is generally bland, but filling; spices are the exception rather than the rule. Protein is often lacking at meals, and meat is generally eaten in small amounts. Pork is usually the meat of choice at holidays and other celebrations.

Estonian food is the most unexciting, with even onions rarely used for flavor. Blood sausage and blood pancakes are a special treat, often served at Christmas. The sausage is prepared with fresh blood, then wrapped in the intestines of a pig. Latvian cooking relies on fermented milk for much of its tang. Smoked foods, such as cheese and fish, are staples in the three countries, as are dairy products and potatoes.

The spiciest foods of the region are found in Lithuania. Over the centuries, spices from the East have made their way into Lithuanian dishes, giving them a more exotic flavor than those of the regions to the north. Delicacies include a traditional dish called *capelinai*. Similar to an Italian *calzone*, *capelinai* is a mound of potato dough filled with either cheese, meat, or mushrooms. It is often topped with a sauce of butter, onions, sour cream, or bacon bits. Vegetables are one of the mainstays of the Baltics. Fresh produce from the garden adorns the cold table, along with cheeses, cream, and an occasional soup.

Breads also play an important part in the Baltic diet, and are a specialty of the region. In Lithuania, many customs relate to the importance of this food. A piece of bread, for example, was placed under the foundation of a new house to ensure that the family never ran out of food. Even today, an important visitor is often greeted with a loaf of fresh bread on a towel.

Baked goods are the most common desserts in the region, with Lithuanian tree cakes being a local favorite. Meals are usually accompanied by tea, coffee, or beer. *Vana Tallinn* is a strong, syrupy sweet liqueur often served with Estonian meals, and *stakliskes* is a favorite Lithuanian honey libation.

Bread is a mainstay of the Baltic diet and plays an important role in the region's cultural traditions.

THE TIMELESS CITIES

The changes that have taken place since independence can be most readily seen in the larger population centers. Cities are growing, evolving units that retain shadows of past generations. The changes that have taken place since independence have added a new layer to Baltic cities and towns.

TALLINN

One of these cities is Tallinn, Estonia's capital and largest city (population 435,000), which lies just fifty-three miles across the Gulf of Finland from Helsinki, Finland's capital. Over the centuries, Tallinn's position as a port on the Baltic Sea has made it a great attraction to other nations. Since its founding at the site of a small Estonian settlement by King Waldemar II of Denmark in 1219, Tallinn (or Reval, the German name by which it was historically known until the twentieth century) has been controlled at one time or another by the Danes, Germans, Swedes, and Russians. It became a member of the Hanseatic League in 1284 and soon established itself as a major center for trade. Because of this cross-cultural history, the city has a unique flavor all its own. Reminders of each of its past rulers can still be seen. The large, uniform, dreary high-rise buildings in the suburbs are the legacy of Russian rule. Evidence of lingering outrage against the Soviets can be seen in a sign posted near a field of ruins near the Niguliste Church. The sign reads, "Tallinn was bombed by the Soviet air forces during the evening and midnight of March 9, 1944. Fifty-three percent of living space was destroyed and 20,000 people lost their homes. 463 people were killed and 659 wounded."[14]

Tallinn consists of three sections: an upper town on a steep hill, a lower walled town, and a new district. Much of the Old Town (Vanalinn) remains, with its winding, cobblestone streets, quaint houses, and high, pointed spires. The hilltop fortress of Toompea (from the German *Domberg*, meaning "Cathedral Hill"), site of the original Estonian settlement, looks out over the gulf. Today, it is home to Riigikogu, the Estonian parliament. According to local legend, the hill also marks the grave of Kalev, the Estonians' mythical ancestor.

Tallinn, Estonia's capital, is a modern-day center of trade and finance, but its medieval historic district reflects the city's colorful past.

CHRISTMAS TREES

Evergreen trees have had symbolic meanings in various cultures since ancient times. Later, the pagan custom of tree worship became popular in many parts of northern Europe. In Germany, the "paradise tree"—a tree with apples hung on it—symbolized the Garden of Eden.

The tradition of decorating a tree for Christmas comes from the Germans, who would bring a paradise tree into their homes around that time of year. The tree would be adorned with wafers, cookies, candles, and other items to celebrate the festive season. The tradition later spread to other parts of Europe and eventually to the United States.

According to some historians, however, the tradition may have actually started in the Baltics. Early-sixteenth-century journals found in Riga relate how local merchants decorated trees on Christmas Eve, then set them on fire after enjoying a joyous meal. Other Estonian writings mention how German knights in Tallinn would decorate a tree carried to the Town Hall square with colorful paper and candles. These historians believe that the tradition was introduced to the German homeland many years later.

In the latter years of the Soviet occupation, foreign capital began to concentrate in Tallinn. Since independence, this trend has accelerated. Today, nearly 90 percent of all foreign money in Estonia is centered in the capital and its surrounding area. Investors have been attracted by the city's communication and transportation systems and its personnel. Baltic neighbor Sweden has led the way in foreign investments.

RIGA

Tallinn is not, however, the largest city in all of the Baltics. That distinction is held by Riga (population 827,000), the capital of Latvia. Riga lies on the Western Dvina River, five miles from where the river empties into the Bay of Riga.

Riga has been the major port in the Baltic region ever since it was founded under Albrecht of Bremen in the early thirteenth century. The generally held belief that whoever ruled Riga ruled the entire Baltic region was one of the main reasons it would be so attractive to Russia in later years. After joining the Hanseatic League in 1282, Riga quickly became one of its main outposts, run by the German nobles and merchants. After becoming part of the Russian Empire, it developed into a major trade and manufacturing center. The effects of the Soviet Russification policy were easily seen. By the time Latvia achieved independence in 1991, a full 70 percent of Riga's population was Russian.

Riga, the capital city of Latvia, has been a critical port and a cultural center for nearly eight hundred years.

Many visitors consider Riga to be the most exciting city in the Baltic States. It has a sense of grandeur and style not found in either of the other capitals. During the period between the two world wars, it was known as "the Paris of the Baltics" because of its lively nightlife and liberal cultural outlook. Arguably the cultural center of the Baltics, Riga today has seen tourism on the increase. This has also caused a rise in related problems, such as traffic congestion and crime.

Old Riga is the city's historic center, surrounded by a moat and containing numerous medieval structures. Many of its buildings were destroyed during the German occupation in World War II, including the Church of St. Peter, which has since been rebuilt. Other buildings have seen changes of another sort. The Russian Orthodox Church, for example, has been reclaimed from its Soviet use as a planetarium during the age of Russification.

VILNIUS

Unlike Tallinn and Riga, which border the Baltic Sea, Vilnius, the capital of Lithuania (population 573,000), is nestled in the southeastern corner of the country, near where the Neris River and Vilnia River meet. Originally settled during the tenth century, it became the capital of Lithuania in 1323 under Grand Duke Gediminas. It has persevered through many calamities over the years, including destruction by the Teutonic Knights, occupation by several nations, fires, plagues, and occupation during the two world wars.

When Vilnius belonged to Poland, its population consisted mainly of Poles and Jews. So prominent was the Jews' role in the life of the city, Vilnius was sometimes referred to as "Northern Jerusalem." The German occupation during World War II destroyed the community and nearly totally eradicated the Jewish population. Today, the Jewish State Museum tells the tragic story of the city's Jewish community. It is the only Jewish museum in the former Soviet Union.

Other reminders of days gone by can still be seen. Many examples of Gothic, Renaissance, baroque, and classical-style architecture may be found along the narrow, cobblestone streets. The ruins of the Castle of Gediminas on Castle Hill still look down over the old town.

OTHER MAJOR CITIES

Independence from Soviet occupation has brought changes to smaller Baltic cities as well. Tartu, the second largest city in Estonia (population 102,000), is found in the southeastern section of the country on the Emajogi River. According to the words of a well-known song, it is the most beautiful city in the republic. Many consider this region to be the "real" Estonia, since the number of non-Estonians is relatively small compared with the rest of the land. Similarly, many refer to Tartu as the "real" capital. The city was founded as Yurev, by Grand Duke Yaroslav of Kiev, in the eleventh century. It later was known by the German name of *Dorpat*. In the thirteenth century, it became a member of the Hanseatic League as an important merchant town. It has been destroyed by invaders and fires several times over the years.

Tartu is the intellectual and educational center of the nation, with Tartu University as its hub. The university was founded (as the Gustavo-Caroline Academy) in 1632 by King Adolphus of Sweden, closed in 1656, then reopened in 1802. Since independence, the university has undergone

The inland city of Vilnius has weathered tremendous adversity since it was named the capital of Lithuania in 1323.

substantial changes. In 1993, the Department of Estonian and Comparative Folklore was reestablished. Since then, the program of folklore studies has expanded significantly. Many new courses have been added, the number of lecturers has increased, and new fields of research have been introduced.

In the seventeenth century, Swedish king Gustavus Adolphus founded the university in Tartu, which has become the educational center of Estonia.

One of the last cities to be affected by the breakup of the Soviet Union is Narva. Lying on the river Narva on the border between Estonia and Russia, it is Estonia's third largest city (population 75,000). It is unique, sitting on the border that divides the East from the West. Because of its position, it has been attractive to Russian rulers over the years. Under Russian control for much of its history, Narva developed into a textile center and an important producer of electric power. A hydroelectric station is located nearby, together with two thermal power stations. Today, Narva's population is more than 90 percent ethnic Russian, a situation that has given rise to troubling questions of ownership of property. The most Russian of Estonian cities, Narva has been slow to surrender some of the embellishments of Soviet occupation. The city was the last to change the old Russian street names. It also had the last remaining statue of Lenin in the Baltic region.

Latvian cities have also changed since 1991. Daugavpils is Latvia's second largest city (population 119,000), nestled in the southeast corner of the country. Lying near the Russian border, the town was an intense subject of Russification. Industries built up by the Soviets, including textiles and the manufacture of bicycles, attracted thousands of Russian immigrants. Today, the city is nearly 90 percent ethnic Russian, and the Latvian language is rarely heard. The industries, however, have suffered greatly as a result of independence.

Liepaja (population 98,000) is a port on Latvia's southwest coast. Founded by the Teutonic Knights in 1263, the city is known as a center of the metallurgy industry and a Russian military base. Because it remained in Russian hands until May 1992, however, economic activity was restricted. Much capital will be needed to adapt the port to commercial use after its decades as a military site. Liepaja holds a special place in Latvian history. It was here in 1919 that the British navy formally recognized the state of Latvia when it disembarked Prime Minister Karlis Ulmanis, who had been forced to flee from Riga. Liepaja was a cradle of the Latvian independence movement of the 1980s and is currently experiencing a revival. It has been named an International City of Change by the World Bank.

As in the other two Baltic nations, independence has brought changes to Lithuanian municipalities. With a population that is

85 percent native Lithuanian, Kaunas has preserved its ethnic heritage more than any other city in the country. It is second to Vilnius in population (411,000) and was Lithuania's temporary capital when Vilnius fell to Poland in 1920. Located at the confluence of the nation's two largest rivers, Kaunas is a melting pot of Lithuanian history and culture. It is the manufacturing center of the region, with textiles and food products among its specialties. In a spirit of cooperation, Kaunas has entered into twinning agreements (the purpose of which is to promote friendship and understanding and stimulate the exchange of knowledge and experience in different fields) with several cities, including Vaxjo, Sweden; Los Angeles, California; Odense, Denmark; Tartu, Estonia; Bialystok, Poland; Grenoble, France; and Tampere, Finland.

The Baltic cities will continue to change in the coming years as their citizens explore the opportunities offered by their newly-won independence. Mistakes will undoubtedly be made, but hopefully the populace will work together to ensure that the cities—and the countries themselves—evolve in a positive direction.

A Tradition Based in Folklore and National Pride

4

A rich tradition of folklore and the struggle for independence have been the two primary influences on Baltic culture. The literature and art that developed over the years owe much to the richness of the practices and customs of the peasants, and to the atmosphere of nationalism that permeated the region.

Folklore

As the fourteenth-century priest Peter of Dusburg noted, the Balts of his day "worship all of creation...sun, moon, stars, thunder, birds, even four-legged creatures down to the toad. They have their sacred forests, fields and waters, in which they do not dare to cut wood, or work, or fish."[15] This ability to see God in nature still characterizes Baltic culture.

When Christianity took root, priests and ministers tried to suppress the folklore, since it dealt with paganism. The pagan festival of Midsummer Night was renamed St. John's Eve for this reason. In the early twentieth century, some people attempted to revive the pagan religions. Although persecuted under Soviet rule, these groups continue their customs to the present day.

Baltic folklore has been able to survive through the centuries largely because of its rich oral tradition of songs and poems. These expressions of what life was like hundreds of years ago cover a variety of subjects. Family life, the peasants' relationship with the land, and ancient myths are all reflected in these tunes and verses.

As far back as 1764, attempts were made to collect examples of these ancient tales. At that time, Johann Herder,

Women in Riga celebrate the festival of Midsummer Night wearing traditional oak wreaths. Ancient folklore closely tied to nature is still a strong influence in Baltic culture.

a German pastor, theorized that a nation's identity is expressed through its traditions and folklore. Thus inspired, Baltic scholars made efforts to record and organize as many of these works as possible. Modernization and the brutal repression under Soviet rule made the task of preserving the folk traditions of the past difficult, but not impossible.

The first guide to Estonian folk stories was published in 1866 by Friedrich Kreutzwald. In Latvia, Krisjanis Barons, an astronomer and mathematician by education, assembled a collection of more than 200,000 folk songs (*dainas*). Most of these songs are four-line poems sung to ancient tunes. They reflect the morals and lifestyles of the ancient Latvians. These lifestyles are further symbolized on holidays and festivals celebrated in the region.

Holidays and Festivals

Many Baltic festivals are based on ancient folklore. Probably the most important celebration commemorates midsummer and the end of spring toil in the fields. It acted as a welcome diversion from the labors of the season. This festival, called *Jaanipaev* in Estonia and *Jani* in Latvia, is rooted deep in the pagan origins of the nations.

One tradition associated with *Jaanipaev* involves leaping over bonfires in the countryside. If the celebrant clears the flames successfully, it is a sign that the coming year will also bring success, both for the people and their livestock. Latvians celebrate *Jani* by gathering around the bonfires, where they eat caraway seed cheese and drink beer brewed especially for the occasion while singing special *Jani* songs. Flowers, grasses, and leaves are gathered to be made into wreaths to decorate the farmsteads.

Singing and dancing are integral parts of Baltic seasonal festivals.

For Estonians, *Jaanipaev* celebrations have been combined with the celebration of *Voidupuha*, or Victory Day. This commemorates June 23, 1919, the day that Estonian forces defeated German troops during the War of Independence. The two holidays have become linked with the same ideals of independence and freedom.

Another observance—*Ziemas Svetki*—marks the Latvian "winter holiday." Revelers sing songs that tell of the sun's return to warm the land once again. Singing and dancing play integral parts in these festivals.

Such festivals are also important in Lithuania. Among the most significant are *Pusiauzemis* (the midwinter festival

SPORTS AND LEISURE

Sports clubs and societies have been part of the Baltic scene since the nineteenth century. Clubs dedicated to hunting, horse riding, yachting, swimming, gymnastics, rowing, skating, cycling, and various winter sports can be found throughout the republics. Vast tracts of unspoiled forest have made hunting one of the biggest attractions. The Latvian Ministry of Forestry organizes parties to shoot wild boar, deer, lynx, fox, and game birds. In Lithuania, the Republican horse races are held each February on frozen Lake Sartu near Utena. Estonia, with its hundreds of islands and miles of coastline, is a favorite destination for yachting. The Tallinn Olympic yachting center was built for the 1980 Moscow Games.

Spectator sports are also popular in the Baltics. Soccer, hockey, and basketball contests routinely draw large crowds. Track-and-field is another favorite, with the Olympics garnering special attention. Since attaining independence, all three nations have been well represented in both the Summer and Winter Games. Prior to 1991, numerous Estonian, Latvian, and Lithuanian athletes won Olympic recognition while representing the Soviet Union. Since the 1992 Winter Games in Albertville, France, they have competed under their own flags. In the 2000 Games in Sydney, Baltic athletes won a total of eleven medals. Erki Nool won a gold medal for Estonia in the men's decathlon, while Igors Vihrovs won a gold for Latvia in gymnastics. Lithuania garnered a total of five medals, including golds for Virgilijus Alekna in the men's discus and Daina Gudzineviciute in women's shooting.

marking the approach of spring), *Uzgavenes* (celebrating the end of winter), *Velykos* (the time of the spring equinox), and *Velines* (the Lithuanian feast for the dead).

ART

The feelings and emotions that inspired the ideals of the region's holidays and festivals also formed the foundation for the body of work produced by Baltic artists over the years.

The earliest works of art to be found in the Baltic region deal with crafts such as woodworking, masonry, weaving, ceramics, and leather working. Animalistic figures and symbols were

Each of the three nations has a sports museum where its top athletes and teams are honored. In recent years, stars in basketball and hockey have turned to the U.S. National Basketball Association and National Hockey League, where they have tested themselves against the best athletes in the world.

Gymnast Igors Vihrovs, competing under the Latvian flag, won a gold medal in the 2000 Olympic Games.

major themes employed by these early artisans. Many grave stones and wooden altars from the thirteenth century can still be seen, often decorated with a combination of pagan and religious symbols (the ring and cross, respectively).

It was not until the middle of the nineteenth century, however, during the National Awakening, that the first Estonian artists of repute made their appearance. Painter Johann Koler and sculptors August Weizenberg and Amandus Adamson are considered the founders of Estonian national art. Koler helped organize a group of Estonian patriots in St. Petersburg in the 1860s. Through his contacts and connections, he was able to protect others in their attempts at bringing about political and cultural reforms. Koler was one of the most prominent artists of his time, known for his portraits of many contemporary personalities.

Weizenberg was the founder of Estonian sculpture. Many of his works are compositions representing figures from mythology. Toward the latter part of the nineteenth century, he produced works portraying prominent Estonian cultural figures. For many natives, his work was their first contact with national art. Adamson made his reputation for his compositions depicting Estonian everyday life. In the 1920s, he produced a series of monuments to the War of Independence.

The national romantic style of painting that eventually developed reflects the themes and legends that abound in the region's folklore. It emphasizes an appreciation for the beauties of nature, an examination of human personality, an exaltation of emotion over reason, an emphasis on imagination, and an interest in folk culture and ethnic cultural origins. This Estonian national romanticism is best exemplified by the work of Ants Laikmaa and Kristjan Raud. Laikmaa is best known for his portraits of the leading figures of the National Awakening. Perhaps the most famous is his painting of Friedrich Kreutzwald, who penned the Estonian national epic *Kalevipoeg*. It became a symbol of the "Young Estonian" movement. Much of Raud's work is based on Estonian folklore. His drawings gave visible form to ancient creatures and natural forces. His name became known to his countrymen through his illustrations for *Kalevipoeg*, and his support of the romantic art ideals of the 1930s.

THE ISLANDS OF ESTONIA

There are approximately fifteen hundred islands lying off the western coast of Estonia in the Baltic Sea. Most are mere points of land, but two are of significant size. More important, they are probably the most unspoiled region of the entire country.

The largest island—Saaremaa—has an area of just over one thousand square miles. Most of the forty-one thousand inhabitants are involved in either working the land or harvesting the sea. There are several sights that attract visitors, including the Kuressaare Episcopal Castle, the only entirely preserved medieval stone castle in the Baltics. Vilsandi National Park, with more than five hundred species of plants, is also found there.

Hiiumaa, the second largest island at 382 square miles, is a favorite spot for Estonian artists and writers. Many have summer retreats there so that they can attend to their craft while enjoying the natural beauty of the unspoiled surroundings.

Ironically, Soviet rule helped preserve the natural environment of the islands. Formerly classified as a frontier zone, the islands were considered strategic outposts, as well as likely points of escape to the West. The only Russians brought to the islands were military people involved with security. Industry was not developed, as it was in many other regions.

Today, the islands are a popular tourist destination. Many natives, however, prefer to retain their relative isolation in order to protect their idyllic way of life.

Around the turn of the twentieth century in Latvia, Rudolfs Perle became known for his romantic style of painting. Janis Valters and Vilhelms Purvitis—considered the creator of Latvian national scenic painting—portrayed elements of Latvian nature in their distinctive landscapes. Janis Rozentals— arguably Latvia's greatest artist ever—gained fame for his stunning portraits and scenes of peasant life. The work of Rozentals marks one of the high points in Latvian art. He is one of the country's most popular painters and one of the founders of the national art school. Many of his works told stories through the use of folklore figures such as fauns and devils. His paintings reflected the emotions of everyday life, ranging from the joyfulness of festivals to the melancholy of times of mourning.

Lithuania's preeminent artist was Mikalojus Ciurlionis, who was also a noted musician. Ciurlionis's personality and attitudes toward the arts were influenced by the cultural and social conditions existing in the early part of the twentieth century. The feelings inspired by the wave of nationalist, patriotic feelings that swept the nation can be seen in his works, including "Past," "The King's Fairy-Tale," and "Altar." The tales and legends related in the folklore of the region were also a source of inspiration for him in works such as "The Prince's Journey," "Ballad," and "Fairy Tale of the Castle."

LITERATURE

Like painting, literature in the Baltics did not emerge until relatively late, delayed as it was by the successive domination of the Germans, Swedes, and Russians. It did not become significant in Estonia and Latvia until the nineteenth century. The oldest body of writings came from Lithuania. Even there, however, works did not appear until much later than literature in other areas of Europe.

The earliest known work printed in Lithuanian was Martynas Mazvydas's *Simple Words of the Catechism* in 1547. Like most Lithuanian writing prior to the eighteenth century, it was a religious text. The first nonreligious work was a 1706 translation of ten of Aesop's fables. Other significant works include the writings of Kristijonas Donelaitis, the "father of Lithuanian literature." The most important, his epic poem *Metai* ("The Seasons"), consists of four parts: "Joys of Spring," "Summer Toils," "Autumn Wealth," and "Winter Cares." The natural setting of Lithuania is portrayed in the poem, as are the nation's people, their work, and their customs. Taken as a whole, *Metai* presents a realistic characterization of eighteenth-century Lithuanian peasant life. In it, Donelaitis accurately depicts the social conditions of the times.

In the first half of the nineteenth century, the University of Vilnius became the center of a literary rebirth. The language and folklore of the country was promoted, leading to a renewed interest in the country's early history. Unfortunately, the Russian czar, fearing a surge in nationalist feelings, banned printing in the Lithuanian language for forty years.

Aesop is illustrated in this fifteenth-century print. In 1706, ten of Aesop's fables were the first nonreligious works to be printed in Lithuanian.

During this period, much Lithuanian literature was published in neighboring East Prussia and smuggled across the border. Motiejus Valancius, a Roman Catholic bishop of Samogitia, was the first to print materials abroad and secretly distribute them. Because of this, his writings on religion and education served to stimulate the emergence of the Lithuanian self-consciousness.

The first modern Lithuanian periodical was published during this period. Folklorist Jonas Basanavicius was the founder and editor of the patriotic newspaper *Ausra* ("The Dawn"), which began publishing in 1883. This journal became known for spreading the romantic ideals of the era. Through its message, *Ausra* rallied many Lithuanians in support of the nationalist movement.

Among the writers at the forefront of this Lithuanian renaissance were poet Vincas Kudirka and poet and dramatist Jonas Maciulis. Kudirka was the founder of the nationalist literary-political periodical *Varpas* ("The Bell"). Printed in Prussia and smuggled into the Russian Empire, *Varpas* became known for its outspoken attacks on Russification policies. Kudirka's satirical writings helped raise the Lithuanian national consciousness. Kudirka is also remembered today as the author of the Lithuanian national anthem.

Maciulis, a Roman Catholic priest known by his pen name of Maironis, is regarded by many as the founder of modern Lithuanian literature. Writing of his love of his country, he put into words the hopes and ambitions of his countrymen. His lyric poetry was published in the collection *Pavasario balsai* ("Voices of Spring").

The ban against printing in Lithuanian was lifted in 1904. Encouraged by the influence of European literary movements and the nation's independence following World War I, Lithuanian writers again looked to the national culture for inspiration. Vincas Kreve-Mickevicius, considered by many to be the greatest Lithuanian writer ever, produced many popular works during this period, including *Dainavos salies senu zmoniu padavimai* ("Old Folks Tales of Dainava"). Many of his stories have their basis in Lithuanian mythology and legends; others are inspired by the plight of rebellious figures.

As in Lithuania, the first known Estonian book was a religious tract, a Lutheran catechism from 1535. The earliest written literature did not appear until the middle of the eighteenth century. The most significant work was the Estonian national epic *Kalevipoeg* ("The Son of Kalev"). This work by Friedrich Reinhold Kreuzwald was the inspiration for the nationalist movement in the country. The story concerns a giant-sized hero who defends his homeland from various invaders. Set in ancient times, it is an allegory for the relationship that existed between the Baltic people and their German conquerors. In time, it came to symbolize the battle against Soviet Russification and the fight for independence. In part, the epic intended to show Estonians that their culture was equal to that of any population.

Another important literary figure of the day was the poet Lydia Koidula, known as the "nightingale of the Emajogi River." She was not only Estonia's best-known literary figure but the daughter of J. V. Jannsen, the publisher of the first Estonian-language newspaper. Koidula was the first author of patriotic poetry in Estonian. Her work praised her native land and was instrumental in strengthening the vision of an independent Estonia among the masses. Thousands of people sang words from her poems at the conclusion of each song festival in Estonia throughout the Russian occupation. She is, arguably, the most influential woman in the nation's history.

In the period between the two world wars, Anton Hansen Tammsaare established a name for himself. The giant of twentieth-century Estonian literature, he is recognized as his country's greatest novelist. His five-volume epic, *Tode ja oigus* ("Truth and Justice"), is considered by many to be the greatest Estonian novel of all time. It depicts the everyday life of a family over the course of three generations, capturing Estonia's evolution from a province in czarist Russia to an independent state. According to the author, the first four of the five volumes deal with man's struggles with the earth, God, society, and himself; the final volume ends with resignation.

Novelist Jaan Kross is one of a new body of writers who have received international recognition. He has been nominated for the Nobel Prize in literature for his historic novels. His most famous work is *The Czar's Madman*, which delves into imperial Russia's relationship with its Baltic province and the problem of maintaining an Estonian identity under foreign rule. By extension, it is an allegory for the authoritarian governments of the modern day.

As in Estonia, Latvian secular literature did not begin to develop until the eighteenth century. At that time, Gottfried Friedrich Stender produced representations of country life that echoed the hundreds of thousands of folk poems of earlier days. It was not until the National Awakening of the nineteenth century, however, that Latvian literature took on a life of its own.

Folk poetry was the inspiration for the writing of Andrejs Pumpurs, whose *Lacplesis* ("Bearslayer") is the Latvian national epic. In many ways, *Lacplesis* is similar to the Estonian epic, *Kalevipoeg.* Both works continue to inspire new generations with their tales of resistance to invasion. The influence of *Lacplesis*, however, seems to be strongest. The Order of Lacplesis has been revived as Latvia's highest award for service to the nation. Kangars, one of the villains of the piece, has become a generic name for traitors. Other character names are given to stores and boutiques; streets also have been named after the epic's hero.

Toward the end of the century, Janis Rainis (pseudonym of Janis Plieksans) burst upon the scene. Considered one of the greatest Latvian writers, Rainis was a poet, translator, and political activist who addressed the contemporary problems of the day. Sometimes referred to as the "Latvian Shakespeare," and acknowledged as the "Man of the 20th Century of Latvia," Rainis also penned a number of popular plays, including *Uguns un Nakts* ("Fire and Night"), a moving testimony to the spirit of the Latvian people, and an inspiration in their struggle for freedom and independence. His wife, Aspazija (Elza Plieksana), also a poet, was an early supporter of feminism.

MUSIC

Baltic music, like its art and literature, has its basis in the folklore of the region. Songs, such as the Latvian *dainas*, played an important role in the pagan rites of centuries ago. Even today, state and public events are often introduced with folk songs that are based on these earlier works.

Certain musical instruments, like the whistle, flute, violin, and zither, are common throughout Eastern Europe. Others are closely associated with individual Baltic nations. The bagpipe is found in Estonia and parts of Latvia, the hammer dulcimer in Lithuania and Latvia, and the bowed harp in Estonia. More unusual instruments, such as the *kokle* (a stringed instrument similar to a zither), *stabule* (a wooden whistle), and *trejdeksnis* (a percussion instrument similar to

SARUNAS MARCIULIONIS

Born in Kaunas, Lithuania, Sarunas Marciulionis first tried his hand at basketball at the age of nine. He became proficient at the sport and joined the *Statyba* team during his years at Vilnius University. Shortly thereafter he was selected for the Soviet junior national squad. At age twenty-three, Marciulionis was a member of the gold medal–winning Soviet Union team at the 1988 Olympics in Seoul, Korea.

On June 23, 1989, Marciulionis became the first Soviet citizen to sign with a team from the National Basketball Association in the United States. He began a successful eight-year pro career, during which he twice finished second in the voting for the "Best NBA Sixth Man." While playing professionally, Marciulionis again participated in the Olympics. As a member of the Lithuanian team, he won a bronze medal in Barcelona in 1992, then repeated the feat in Atlanta in 1996.

Despite his successful playing career, Marciulionis has made even more of a name for himself since his retirement. He has devoted much of his time, energy, and money to the Sarunas Lithuanian Children's Fund to help youngsters in his native land. He is the owner of the Sarunas Hotel in Vilnius, where he founded a private basketball school. Marciulionis is also the founder and commissioner of the Northern European Basketball League, a group of fourteen teams that began play in 2000. As a result of his talent and dedication to his country, Marciulionis has been named the most popular sportsman in Lithuania four times.

a metal rattle), may also be heard. Among the most popular modern instruments are the accordion and guitar.

Rudolf Tobias composed Estonia's first symphonic work, his overture *Julius Caesar*. He also wrote Estonia's first piano sonata, oratorio, and polyphonic compositions. Included among his other creative goals was the musical incarnation of *Kalevipoeg*, the Estonian national epic. Unfortunately, he did not live long enough to carry out this plan.

Veljo Tormis and Alo Mattiisen are two of the biggest names in modern Estonian music. Tormis helped revive the ancient chanting-style song called the runic. In Estonian culture, choral music has had a significant role in the nationalist movement; amateur choruses perform at the National

*In Latvia and
Lithuania, traditional
music is often played on
the hammer dulcimer.*

Song Festival every five years. Tormis's colorful, orchestral style of writing for voices creates tensions with the repetition of ancient folk tunes. His first great cycle "Estonian Calendar Songs" for a male and a female chorus demonstrate the enchanting power of ancient folk tunes used as the material for original choral songs. Mattiisen was a pop music composer recognized as the songwriter of Estonia's independence. He became a national hero by writing some of the most dramatic and inspirational songs of the Singing Revolution. His musical style combined a rock compositional flair with purely keyboard compositions.

The name that dominates the field of music in Lithuania is Mikalojus Konstantinas Ciurlionis. In the span of a short, thirty-six-year life, he composed approximately three hundred works. The tone of his creations reflected the political and cultural conditions existing in Lithuania at the beginning of the twentieth century. These are expressed in his symphonic poems *In the Forest* and *The Sea*, his choral compositions, and his piano pieces. In the poems, man communicates with nature, himself being an integral part of it. The images of Lithuanian forests, together with the calm grandeur of the sea, merge into one memorable experience. As a Lithuanian, the character in the poems feels the bonds linking him to his native land, giving him a feeling of his place in the universe. Choral pieces and reworkings of folk songs are part of Ciurlionis's contribution to Lithuanian culture. "The melodies born in human soul," wrote Ciurlionis, "are most impressive and enchanting, like our genuine ancient songs."[16]

Music Festivals

Music played an important role in the pagan rituals of the early Balts. This love has been carried down to the present

A Most Unusual Memorial

Frank Zappa, of the Mothers of Invention singing group, had many fans around the world. Known for his antiestablishment songs, he even had a fan club in Lithuania. When Zappa died of cancer in 1993, the president of the club decided to do something. Thirty-one-year-old Lithuanian photographer Saulius Paukstys wanted to see if his newly-independent country was as democratic as it claimed. He petitioned the city government for permission to build a bust of Zappa outside of the Vilnius art academy.

Zappa had no connection to Lithuania whatsoever, never even having visited the country. Nevertheless, the authorities did not reject the project—they only objected to having to pay for it. Paukstys and his friends helped raise one thousand dollars for the memorial, a stone bust atop a four-meter-high stainless steel column. Although the memorial was placed near the Vilnius city center (teachers at the art academy feared the effect the monument would have on the minds of the impressionable young students), the work by seventy-year-old sculptor Konstantinas Bogdanas was completed and unveiled in late 1996.

day in the form of folk festivals. In his journal *Ausra*, Basanavicius characterized folk songs as a national wealth destined to call the nation to struggle for a better future. This is exactly what they did. The festivals were one of the few ways the national spirit could be kept alive through the years of Soviet rule. The outpouring of feelings came to be known as the Singing Revolution.

In Estonia, music festivals date back to 1869. Aware of the Estonian's love of singing, Russian authorities saw no harm in allowing a festival of song to be staged that year near Tartu. Estonian leaders recognized the possibilities such a gathering presented. The festivals soon became a meeting place where the nationalist movement was engendered. Since then, they have grown larger and larger. In 1990, at the height of the push for independence, the National Song Festival (held every five years) attracted an audience of some 300,000 people. Thousands of people perform at these festivals, which are basically huge national choir events. Other popular gatherings include the annual Rock Festival, the International Organ Music Festival, the Jazz and Blues Festival, and the Viljandi Folk Music Festival. Latvia and Lithuania hold similar festivals during the course of the year.

FILM

The latest art to find inspiration in the Baltic struggle for independence is film. Originally established in the 1940s, the movie industry is experiencing a rebirth in the Baltic nations. An influx of foreign money has helped bring the cinema into the modern age. Movie houses throughout the area show the latest Western releases, and several documentaries and shorts produced in the region have garnered international acclaim.

In Estonia, Mark Soosaar is the foremost documentary maker, and the founder of the Charlie Chaplin Cultural Center in Pärnu. He is known for analyzing the changes that have occurred in the nation by focusing on the lives of unforgettable characters. One such film—*Mission Impossible*—focuses on nationalist leaders Ernst Jaakson, Estonia's ambassador to the United Nations, and Trivimi Velliste, the country's foreign minister, as they work to eliminate war and hatred. Lennart Meri, the current president of Estonia, was also a

Opera and Ballet

In a region where singing is such an important part of the heritage, it is not surprising that opera is loved as well. Such is the case in Estonia. Unfortunately, there is only one opera house in the country—the Estonia Theater. Many attribute the sad state of the art to poor direction, and the tendency of newcomers to look outside the nation for opportunities that do not exist in Estonia. In Latvia, Andrejs Zagars has been a driving force behind the revival of opera, as was Jazeps Vitols, who founded the National Opera and the state conservatory.

Most performances in the Baltic region tend to be classical. More funding and an infusion of new blood is needed to bring the discipline into the twenty-first century.

Ballet is in a much better state. For years, Riga had an excellent reputation in the realm of ballet, ranking behind only the Kirov and Bolshoi in quality. The great Mikhail Baryshnikov, among others, trained in the Latvian capital. Ballet is also an important part of Lithuanian culture. Many outstanding dancers come out of the Vilnius School of Choreography and the Kaunas School of Music.

Students at the Vilnius School in Lithuania hope to carry on the Baltic tradition of excellence in ballet.

THE *MS ESTONIA* DISASTER

In late 2000, word leaked out that Hollywood was reportedly planning a major movie on the sinking of the *MS Estonia*. The tragedy—Europe's worst maritime disaster since World War II—has been the subject of much speculation.

The *Estonia* was a symbol of the nation's newfound self-confidence. The fifteen-thousand-ton white ferry regularly shuttled passengers between Tallinn and Stockholm. In the early morning hours of September 28, 1994, something went dreadfully wrong. At the midway point of its journey, the ship encountered a storm. It sank to the bottom of the Baltic Sea, with 852 of the 989 people on board going down with it.

The official investigation into the disaster laid the blame on poorly built bow door locks that gave way when the ship was hit by powerful waves. Others have posed more dramatic theories. Some suggested that the boat was deliberately sunk by members of organized crime in order to conceal contraband that was being smuggled. Another theory proposed an explosion caused by secret Swedish military weapons that were on board. Still others thought the boat might have hit a Russian submarine. Although the truth may never be known, it is certain that the event will never be forgotten by the families whose lives were touched by the disaster.

film director of note. His films on Finno-Ugric tribes in the USSR won him renown in the 1970s and '80s.

Latvia's most famous filmmaker was Juris Podnieks. Trained at the Moscow Film School and apprenticed at the Riga Film Studios, he made his first major documentary in 1982. His films include *Hello, Do You Hear Us?*—which examined life in the Soviet Union—and *Is It Easy to Be Young?*—a look at the alienation and despair of Soviet youth. His film *Homeland*, a tribute to his native country, included scenes from the Soviet attack on Riga in 1991. His two cameramen were among the five people killed that night. The film is an inspiring record of the outpouring of feeling accompanying folk festivals in Latvia, Estonia, and Lithuania.

The arts in the Baltic nations developed at a much slower pace than in other European countries. Now that independence has eliminated the state backing for the arts that existed under Soviet rule, another obstacle remains to be overcome. In the past, writers, painters, and musicians have been able to encourage action through their creative energy. The hope is that they will continue to do so in the future.

5

FACING THE NEW MILLENNIUM

In December 1991, most of the republics of the former Soviet Union formed an association called the Commonwealth of Independent States (CIS). The three Baltic nations declined to join, fearing that Russia would control the group. They had no intention of putting themselves back in the same situation they had struggled so hard to escape.

After gaining their independence, Estonia, Latvia, and Lithuania had to dig themselves out from under the rubble that came about from Soviet rule. To do so, they had to install governments capable of leading them into the future and solving problems that were of immediate concern. The economies were in chaos, with prices spiraling out of control; thousands of Communist troops remained stationed at military bases throughout the region; the status of the Russian immigrants needed to be addressed; and much of the environment had been devastated by the effects of Soviet occupation. How Estonia, Latvia, and Lithuania faced these problems would determine the course of the new nations' futures.

GOVERNMENT

Each of the three Baltic nations has made the transition from a Communist system of government to a multiparty parliamentary democracy. There are many similarities between the three republics.

In Estonia, the legislative power rests with a state assembly (Riigikogu). Each of the 101 members is elected to a four-year term. These representatives elect a president of the republic to a five-year term of office. As chief of state, the president is responsible for the general domestic policy of the nation. A prime minister is appointed by the president and shares executive power with the Council of Ministers.

The legislature is a coalition, with no one party holding a majority.

Latvia's one-hundred-member unicameral (consisting of one body) legislature is the Saeima, also a coalition of parties. Delegates serve four-year terms. The president of the republic is elected by the legislature, and the president selects the prime minister, who acts as the head of the government.

The same general system applies in Lithuania. The president of the republic, however, is elected to a five-year term by popular vote. The prime minister is the head of government, appointed by the president and confirmed by the

Leaders of the democratic Baltic nations, like Estonian president Lennart Meri, had to revitalize their countries after years of Soviet rule.

VAIRA VIKE-FREIBERGA

On July 8, 1999, Vaira Vike-Freiberga was sworn in as Latvia's second president since the country regained its independence in 1991. She is the first female head of state in Eastern Europe.

Born in Latvia, Vike-Freiberga fled with her family to Canada when the Soviets invaded at the close of World War II. She was trained as a psychologist and has served as president of the Canadian Psychological Association and the Social Science Federation of Canada. She is also a linguist who speaks English, French, German, Latvian, and Spanish fluently.

After living in Canada and Europe for more than fifty years, Vike-Freiberga returned to her homeland in 1998. Even while abroad, she had been active in the Latvian community, regularly addressing Latvian educational seminars. On a more personal level, she and her husband have compiled an impressive collection of *dainas* (traditional Latvian folk songs).

Since her return, Vike-Freiberga has directed the Latvian Institute, which works to promote Latvia's name on an international level. As Mel Huang reported in the *Central European Review*, at her inauguration she articulated her feelings on her people's role in the modern age: "We are the inheritors of our past, but we are not slaves who should live in the shadow of our past. We are the builders of our own future."

Latvian president Vaira Vike-Freiberga was the first female head of state in Eastern Europe.

parliament (Seimas). Each of the legislature's 141 members serves for a period of four years. Seventy-one of the seats are elected by popular vote, while the other seventy are awarded proportionately to the various political parties.

Over the past decade, the governments have faced their fair share of problems and growing pains. Scandals involving bribery, illegal surveillance, and the privatization of real estate have surfaced and been resolved. Among the most pressing issues has been the improvement of health care and social services.

HEALTH AND SOCIAL SERVICES

The health care systems inherited from the Russian regime, mainly state owned and operated, were not up to the standards of those in Western nations, although they did surpass those in the other Russian republics. The life expectancy has dropped somewhat in the Baltics, in part due to deteriorating living standards; it currently stands at about sixty-five for men and seventy-five for women. Cardiovascular disease is the number one cause of death, with cancer and accidents also ranking high. Although the number of doctors, dentists, and hospital beds per thousand people is relatively high by Soviet standards, problems still abound. There is a dire shortage of nurses, medical equipment, supplies, and drugs.

The social welfare systems also have far to go to reach the level of Western nations. The governments have instituted plans to provide support for invalids, low-income families, families with three or more children, and the elderly. The largest portion of funds, however, goes toward pensions. With a rapidly aging population, the amount received by pensioners is generally less than what is required for a comfortable standard of living. To partially alleviate this problem, Estonia gradually raised the retirement age from fifty-five for women and sixty for men to sixty and sixty-five, respectively. A more satisfactory solution to the problem remains to be seen.

Life is far less predictable than it was during the Russian regime. Some people find that hard to accept. For the majority, however, the uncertainty of life is a welcome change, bringing with it opportunities never before possible. Many of these lie in the economic sector.

STABILIZING THE ECONOMY

One of the main problems facing the Baltic States was rein-
vigorating economies that had been crippled by the Soviet
move to integrate them into the USSR's centrally planned
structure. In an effort to get the economy back on track, Estonia replaced the Russian ruble with its own national currency, the kroon, in June 1992. Latvia and Lithuania took
similar actions within the year, Latvia introducing the lat and
Lithuania, the litas. Since then, the three currencies have remained relatively stable.

Under Soviet rule, Estonia enjoyed more prosperity than
other regions of the USSR. This came about mainly through
the development of industries involving the country's natural resources. The republic's oil shale and phosphorites
were a major source of energy for much of the Soviet Empire.

After independence, Estonia's economy was reorga-
nized along free-market principles (in which most of a
country's wealth—its land and natural resources, machines
and factories, personal and consumer goods, and cash and
securities—is held in private ownership by many different
individuals, corporations, and other nongovernmental organizations). Most businesses have become privately
owned as the nation has moved away from government
control. As inefficient state enterprises were privatized,
the economy began to thrive.

Estonia has improved its economic ties with the Western
European nations and moved away from Russia. It signed a
free-trade agreement with Latvia and Lithuania in 1993. The
pact removed duties on imports between the three Baltic
nations.

Success in economic matters has enabled Estonia to establish itself on the world stage. It has attracted more foreign
investment than its neighbors. In 1996, the Daiwa Institute
of Research called the Estonian economy "a tiger in the making."[17] Latvia and Lithuania have also progressed since
achieving independence, but not as rapidly.

Latvia's transformation into a market economy has been
second to Estonia's. Much of the nation's industry has been
privatized. Tough reform policies have helped keep inflation
in check while the private sector has developed. The country's strategic location on the Baltic Sea has been a boost to
its economic recovery. It has also, however, created prob-

lems. One such problem concerned fishing and oil-drilling rights. The dispute was resolved with the ratification of treaties that demarcated the sea borders between the three Baltic nations.

Lithuania has made steady progress in its move toward developing a market economy, although somewhat slower

The natural resources of the Baltics include oil shale, which has provided a major source of energy for the region.

The seaports of the Baltic States, like Tallinn in Estonia, have been crucial in rebuilding the nations' economies.

than Estonia and Latvia. Inflation, for example, has been higher than in the other Baltic republics. Lithuania's industrial sector is in the process of being privatized, with many large industries still under state control. The nation's economic recovery is benefited by its location. The city of Vilnius is a rail and highway hub that connects the country with Eastern Europe, Belarus, Russia, and Ukraine. The ice-free port of Klaipeda on the Baltic Sea is another plus. Ships can be loaded and unloaded twenty-four hours a day, in any season of the year.

The importance of adequate systems of transportation and communication cannot be underestimated. In order to continue their journey toward economic recovery, the Baltics must continue to work with each other. Maintaining that balance will be a key element in their struggle. As Latvian Transport Minister Vilis Kristopans said, "We cannot have extremely poor political relations and at the same time enjoy very good economic relations."[18] Nowhere is this more important than in the nations' dealings with Russia.

RELATIONS WITH RUSSIA

Since the Baltic States won their independence in 1991, their relations with Russia have centered around several issues. The withdrawal of Russian troops, the citizenship status of Russians living in the Baltic republics, border disputes, and national security are among the most important.

Immediately upon gaining autonomy, Estonia, Latvia, and Lithuania began insisting that Russia remove its troops stationed in the three nations. Russia pressed for more time, arguing that there was no place for the forces to go. The Estonian government agreed to guarantee the rights of the military personnel living in their nation. Latvia agreed to allow the Russians to lease the Skrunda radar base for five years in return for evacuating their troops. By 1994, all other foreign forces stationed in the three countries had been withdrawn.

The question of Russian citizenship was a stickier issue. With ethnic Russians making up approximately 30 percent of Estonia's population and 34 percent of Latvia's, the challenge was how to integrate these communities, whose loyalty to the newly independent states was uncertain. (The situation was not as severe in Lithuania, where ethnic Lithuanians made up approximately 80 percent of the population.)

Under new citizenship policies, the Estonian and Latvian governments decided that the ethnic Russians had no automatic right to citizenship. In order to qualify for naturalization, they had to meet certain strict requirements, including residency for a specific number of years and fluency in the native language. Russia responded by making accusations of human rights violations. In an effort to improve relations, citizenship requirements have been eased somewhat since 1992.

Russia and Estonia also continue to be locked in a border dispute. According to the 1920 Tartu Peace Treaty, Estonia's border extended past the Narva River in the northeastern portion of the country, and beyond the town of Petseri in the southeast. Stalin, however, incorporated this region into Russia following World War II. The Estonians continue to claim the land as theirs, but Russia refuses to give in. The Yeltsin government refused to accept responsibility for acts committed by the Soviets.

A Russian soldier stands guard at a rail checkpoint between Russia and Estonia in 1935. Continuing disputes with Russia include conflicting claims to lands on the Estonian border.

This constant reminder of Russian occupation makes it difficult for Balts to ignore their neighbor to the east. National security is a vital issue to the Baltic States, as it is for every nation. Having defied the Russians in gaining their independence, the three nations are ever wary of another attempt at subjugation by their former rulers. With this in mind, Estonia, Latvia, and Lithuania attempted to join the North Atlantic Treaty Organization (NATO). NATO is an international organization whose member nations agree to resolve disputes among themselves peacefully and to defend one another against outside aggressors. Thus far, however,

Sea Mines

The waterways in the Baltics were supply routes for the Nazis and Soviets during World War II. Over time, the Germans, Russians, British, and Swedes laid approximately eighty-five thousand mines in the area. Clean-ups after the war were haphazard at best, and it is estimated that nearly thirty thousand mines still remain, making the region the most heavily mined waters in the world.

According to authorities, the mines do not pose a major problem. The main shipping lanes have long been cleared, and there have been no reported incidents of ships being damaged due to exploding mines. Many are so old and rusted, they are no longer active. The Baltic governments, however, would rather take no chances. Danger still exists: An unexploded mine could be snagged in a fisherman's net or washed ashore along the coastline.

The Swedish navy has been responsible for finding the majority of mines, using radar to search them out. Dolphins have also been tried, but with less success. The Baltic governments are still attempting to investigate every waterway and bay in the area. With more than twenty-three hundred miles of winding coastline and more than one thousand islands in Estonia alone, it is a job that will likely take many more years to complete.

Specially trained dolphins have been used to locate unexploded World War II mines in Baltic waterways.

NATO has only shown a willingness to aid the three nations in an advisory capacity. Membership remains a Baltic objective, despite Russian threats to take measures to prevent it.

SAVING THE ENVIRONMENT

Trying to undo the damage done to the environment over the course of nearly a half-century of Soviet rule is a major problem facing the Baltic nations. The development of industry during the Soviet regime had a dramatic impact on the three countries.

Two power plants located near Narva in Estonia supply much of the power of both Latvia and northwestern Russia.

Industrial waste from facilities like this chemical plant in Estonia has had a devastating effect on the environment.

The electricity produced is generated by power plants fired with oil shale. Estonia is one of the world's leading producers of oil shale. Unfortunately, the process in which this material is burned produces disastrous side effects. The air is heavily polluted with sulfur dioxide emissions from the plants, and the mining process itself has damaged groundwater in the region.

In addition, the soil and groundwater have also been contaminated by the chemicals and petroleum products used and discarded by Russian military bases. Over the years, hundreds of thousands of tons of jet fuel have been dumped into the ground, and toxic chemicals and explosives have found their way into the water.

In Latvia, the Western Dvina and Lielupe Rivers empty into Riga Bay near Jurmala. The Western Dvina is so heavily polluted with industrial waste that swimmers often emerge from its waters with skin rashes and infections. The waste is carried far from its point of origin to areas where it can harm unsuspecting inhabitants. Children who walk along the river shores in search of pieces of amber may instead pick up a chunk of water-borne phosphorus disgorged from a plant many miles away and burn their fingers.

The Baltic Sea, the lifeline of trade in the region and the center of its fishing industry, is also in serious trouble. Industrial waste and untreated sewage have poured into the sea, drastically reducing the flora and fauna that live there. Since the sea is a shallow body of water with a slow current, the wastes are not easily flushed away. The effects of decades of dumping can still be seen.

Much of the industrial pollution is a by-product of the processes that produce much-needed energy. The oil-shale industry continues to be a major threat, producing mountains of hazardous waste compounds that are eventually washed away into the sea. When the oil shale supplies run out within the next century, the Baltics will likely turn more to nuclear energy. The region has already had firsthand experience with the dangers involved. Fallout from the 1986 nuclear explosion at the Chernobyl power plant in Ukraine passed over the three nations.

The damage caused by the oil-shale industry and the explosion at Chernobyl heightened the general population's awareness of dangers to the environment. When news of a

THE IGNALINA NUCLEAR POWER PLANT

The disaster at the Chernobyl power plant in Ukraine in 1986 warned the world of the dangers of nuclear power. The explosion in a nuclear reactor released radiation equal to about two hundred times the combined radiation from the two atomic bombs the United States dropped during World War II. Since Chernobyl, other plants have come under intense scrutiny in hopes of preventing a similar disaster. According to most experts, the Ignalina Nuclear Power Plant in Lithuania is one of the major sources of concern. Ignalina's reactor No. 1 is the largest Chernobyl-type reactor of the sixteen located in the territory of the former Soviet Union.

Much about the plant is outdated or in a state of disrepair. Many safety features are manual and prone to glitches. Perhaps most upsetting is the lack of containment shells around the reactors. Those in charge say this feature is not necessary because the water piping system is adequate. The facility seems to be tempting fate, and several problems have occurred over the years. In October 1992, a crack in the reactor cooling system almost caused a major accident. Crows landing on power lines have caused alarms to go off and caused temporary shutdowns. And in a startling breach of security, a cleaning lady found a grenade in a men's toilet near one of the reactors in 1999.

Unfortunately, repairs and improvements cost money. It is estimated that the cost to keep the plant running safely—approximately one billion dollars—is the same as the amount needed to shut it down. The problem must be addressed at some point in the future. The consequences for the environment could be dire if it is ignored.

plan to build a hydroelectric plant on the Western Dvina River in Latvia was made public, more than thirty thousand people signed petitions in protest. The project was canceled the next year. Similarly, a large-scale plan to mine phosphate deposits in eastern Estonia caused a huge public outcry when it was revealed in 1987. The threat to the groundwater in this most fertile part of the country gave rise to numerous protests.

In Lithuania, a nuclear power plant in Ignalina stirred fear in the populace since it was the same type as the one in Chernobyl. Two reactors are currently in operation, but plans for another two were halted when ecological and pro-independence groups staged demonstrations against them.

The protest movement in the three nations proved crucial in furthering the growth of national consciousness across the Baltic region. Said Rapolas Liuzinas of Lithuania's Environmental Protection Department, "The protest about the environment was a kind of protest against the government. It made people realize they are hosts in their own land and shouldn't accept the dictates of others."[19]

That philosophy is the guiding principle for the three Baltic nations as they endeavor to find their place in the world of the twenty-first century. Having been forced to submit to the vagaries of Russian rule for many decades, it would be easy for the Balts to sit back and accept the status quo. Like a child going off to college, however, they must learn to take responsibility for making their own decisions, for determining the course their future will take. The process is not an easy one, but neither was the job of preserving a culture through centuries of foreign domination. The three Baltic nations have been able to do that. They are well on their way to making their mark in the new millennium.

FACTS ABOUT THE BALTICS

ESTONIA

Demography

Population (1998): 1,447,000.

Density (1998): persons per sq. mi., 88.4; persons per sq. km., 34.1.

Urban-rural (1996): urban, 69.4%; rural, 30.6%.

Sex distribution (1996): male, 47.23%; female, 52.77%.

Age breakdown (1995): under 15, 20.7%; 15–29, 21.0%; 30–44, 21.7%; 45–59, 18.1%; 60–74, 13.8%; 75 and over, 4.7%.

Population projection: (2000) 1,421,000; (2010) 1,351,000.

Ethnic composition (1994): Estonian, 63.9%; Russian, 29.0%; Ukrainian, 2.7%; Belarusian, 1.6%; Finnish, 1.0%; other, 1.8%.

Religious affiliation (1995): Christian, 38.1% (of which, Evangelical Lutheran, 19.6% and Estonian Orthodox, 13.7%); other (mostly nonreligious), 61.9%.

Major cities (1996): Tallinn, 434,763; Tartu, 101,901; Narva, 75,211; Kohtla-Järve, 68,533; Pärnu, 51,807.

Vital Statistics

Birth rate per 1,000 population (1996): 9.0; (1994) legitimate, 59.1%; illegitimate, 40.9%.

Death rate per 1,000 population (1996): 12.9.

Natural increase rate per 1,000 population (1996): –3.9.

Total fertility rate (avg. births per childbearing woman; 1995): 1.3.

Marriage rate per 1,000 population (1994): 4.9.

Divorce rate per 1,000 population (1994): 3.7.

Life expectancy at birth (1993): male, 62.4 years; female, 73.8 years.

Major causes of death per 100,000 population (1993): diseases of the circulatory system, 792.9; cancers, 225.3; accidents, 110.5.

National Economy

Production (metric tons except as noted):

Agriculture, forestry, fishing (1996): potatoes, 500,000; barley, 273,000; oats, 100,000; wheat, 100,000; rye, 70,000; apples, 17,000; livestock (number of live animals), 449,000 pigs; 370,400 cattle; roundwood (1996), 3,901,000 cu. m.; fish catch (1995), 212,000.

103

Mining and quarrying (value of production in Estonian kroon '000,000; 1994): oil shale, 781; peat, 121.

Manufacturing (value of production in Estonian kroon '000,000; 1994): meat and meat products, 1,502; chemicals and chemical products, 1,502; dairy products, 1,368; fish and fish products, 1,156; beverages, 1,091; cement, bricks, and tiles, 923; wood and wood products (excluding furniture), 922; textiles, 908.

Household income and expenditure:

Average household size (1994), 3.1; average net income per household (1994), Estonian kroon 46,303 (US$3,681).

Sources of income (1994): wages and salaries, 53.0%; transfers, 12.8%; self-employment, 5.7%; other, 28.5%.

Expenditure (1994): food and beverages, 41.0%; housing, 9.6%; transportation, 9.2%; clothing and footwear, 8.4%.

Gross national product (1996): US$4,509,000,000 (US$3,080 per capita).

Tourism (1995): receipts, US$353,000,000; expenditures, US$90,000,000.

Land use (1994): forest, 44.7%; pasture, 7.2%; agriculture, 32.2%; other, 15.9%.

Foreign Trade

Imports (1996): mineral fuels and chemical products, 23.4%; electrical and nonelectrical machinery, 21.9%; foodstuffs, 15.6%.

Major import sources: Finland, 36.2%; Russia, 12.9%; Germany, 8.9%.

Exports (1996): mineral fuels and chemical products, 18.1%; foodstuffs, 16.1%; textiles and clothing, 14.4%; wood and paper products, 12.6%.

Major export destinations: Finland, 18.3%; Russia, 16.7%; Sweden, 11.4%; Latvia, 8.4%; Germany, 7.0%.

Transport

Railroads (1996): route length, 1,018 km.; (1995) passenger-km., 421,000,000; metric ton-km. cargo, 3,612,000,000.

Roads (1995): total length, 14,992 km. (paved, 54%).

Vehicles (1995): passenger cars, 383,000; trucks and buses, 96,700.

Merchant marine (1992): vessels (100 gross tons and over), 234; (1994) total deadweight tonnage, 695,000.

Air transport (1996): passenger-km., 120,000,000; metric ton-km. cargo, 762,000; airports (1997), 1.

Education and Health

Educational attainment (1989): percentage of population age 25 and over having no formal schooling, 2.2%; primary education, 39.0%; secondary, 45.1%; higher, 13.7%.

Literacy (1989): percentage of population age 15 and over literate, 99.7%; males literate, 99.9%; females literate, 99.6%.

Health (1994): physicians, 4,680 (1 per 319 persons); hospital beds, 12,521 (1 per 119 persons); (1996) infant mortality rate per 1,000 live births, 12.1.

Military

Total active duty personnel (1997): 3,510 (army, 95.4%; navy, 4.6%).

Military expenditure as percentage of GNP (1995): 1.1% (world, 2.8%); per capita expenditure, US$80.

LATVIA

Demography

Population (1998): 2,445,000.

Density (1998): persons per sq. mi., 98.0; persons per sq. km., 37.8.

Urban-rural (1996): urban, 69.0%; rural, 31.0%.

Sex distribution (1996): male, 46.3%; female, 53.7%.

Age breakdown (1996): under 15, 20.4%; 15–29, 20.3%; 30–44, 21.5%; 45–59, 18.5%; 60–74, 14.3%; 75 and over, 5.0%.

Population projection: (2000) 2,394,000; (2010) 2,214,000.

Ethnic composition (1996): Latvian, 55.1%; Russian, 32.6%; Belarusian, 4.0%; Ukrainian, 2.9%; Polish, 2.2%; Lithuanian, 1.3%; other, 1.9%.

Religious affiliation (1995): Christian, 39.6% (of which, Protestant, 16.7%; Roman Catholic, 14.9%; Orthodox, 8.0%); Jewish, 0.6%; other (mostly nonreligious), 59.8%.

Major cities (1996): Riga, 826,508; Daugavpils, 118,530; Liepaja, 98,490; Jelgava, 70,957; Jurmala, 59,002.

Vital Statistics

Birth rate per 1,000 population (1996): 7.9; (1994) legitimate, 73.6%; illegitimate, 26.4%.

Death rate per 1,000 population (1996): 13.8.

Natural increase rate per 1,000 population (1996): –5.9.

Total fertility rate (avg. births per childbearing woman; 1996): 1.2.

Marriage rate per 1,000 population (1995): 4.4.

Divorce rate per 1,000 population (1995): 3.2.

Life expectancy at birth (1996): male, 60.8 years; female, 73.2 years.

Major causes of death per 100,000 population (1994): diseases of the circulatory system, 917.0; accidents, poisoning, and violence, 235.9; cancers, 219.6; diseases of the respiratory system, 52.8.

National Economy

Production (metric tons except as noted):

Agriculture, forestry, fishing (1996): potatoes, 900,000; barley, 384,000; wheat, 306,000; sugar beets, 245,000; vegetables and melons, 232,000; fruits and berries, 91,000; livestock (number of live animals); 553,000 pigs; 537,000 cattle; 72,100 sheep; 3,500,000 poultry; roundwood (1995), 6,907,000 cu. m.; fish catch (1995), 149,719.

Mining and quarrying (1996): peat, 462,700; gypsum, 77,226.

Manufacturing (value added in US$'000,000; 1994): food products, 193; beverages, 76; transport equipment, 59; wood and wood products, 56; electrical machinery, 42; textiles, 41; nonelectrical machinery, 39.

Household income and expenditure:

Average household size (1989), 3.1.

Sources of income (1994): wages and salaries, 67.0%; pensions and transfers, 17.4%; self-employment, 5.4%; other, 10.2%.

Expenditure (1995): food and beverages, 44.2%; housing and energy, 14.1%; clothing and footwear, 8.1%; transport and communications, 7.8%; recreation and education, 6.3%.

Gross national product (1996): US$5,730,000,000 (US$2,300 per capita).

Land use (1994): forested, 44.4%; meadows and pastures, 12.4%; agricultural and under permanent cultivation, 27.0%; other, 16.2%.

Foreign Trade

Imports (1996): mineral products, 22.2%; machinery and equipment, 16.8%; chemicals and chemical products, 11.0%; textiles, 8.0%; base metals, 6.4%.

Major import sources: Russia, 20.2%; Germany, 13.8%; Finland, 9.2%; Sweden, 7.9%; Lithuania, 6.3%.

Exports (1996): forestry products, 24.4%; textiles, 16.9%; food and agricultural products, 16.4%; machinery and apparatus, 9.7%.

Major export destinations: Russia, 22.8%; Germany, 13.8%; United Kingdom, 11.1%; Lithuania, 7.4%; Sweden, 6.6%.

Transport

Railroads (1996): length, 2,413 km.; passenger-km., 1,182,000,000; metric-km. cargo, 12,412,000,000.

Roads (1993): total length, 64,693 km. (paved, 18.2%).

Vehicles (1996): passenger cars, 379,895; trucks and buses, 90,184.

Merchant marine (1992): cargo vessels, 261; total deadweight tonnage, 1,436,899.

Air transport (1996): passenger-km., 301,500,000; metric ton-km. cargo, 5,201,000; airports with scheduled flights (1996), 1.

Education and Health

Educational attainment (1988): percentage of population age 25 and over having no formal schooling, 0.6%; incomplete primary education, 18.5%; complete primary education, 21.2%; secondary, 46.3%; higher, 13.4%.

Literacy (1989): percentage of total population age 15 and over literate, 99.5%.

Health (1995): physicians, 8,400 (1 per 298 persons); hospital beds, 27,800 (1 per 90 persons); infant mortality rate per 1,000 live births (1996), 15.9.

Military

Total active duty personnel (1997): 8,100 (border guard, 44.4%; army, 42.0%; navy, 12.1%; air force, 1.5%).

Military expenditure as percentage of GNP (1995): 0.9% (world, 2.8%); per capita expenditure, US $29.

LITHUANIA

Demography

Population (1998): 3,704,000.

Density (1998): persons per sq. mi., 146.9; persons per sq. km., 56.7.

Urban-rural (1996): urban, 67.8%; rural, 32.2%.

Sex distribution (1996): male, 47.22%; female, 52.78%.

Age breakdown (1996): under 15, 21.6%; 15–29, 22.0%; 30–44, 22.1%; 45–59, 16.9%; 60–69, 9.7%; 70 and over, 7.7%.

Population projection: (2000) 3,702,000; (2010) 3,639,000.

Ethnic composition (1996): Lithuanian, 81.6%; Russian, 8.2%; Polish, 6.9%; Belarusian, 1.5%; Ukrainian, 1.0%; other, 0.8%.

Religious affiliation (1995): Roman Catholic, 72.2%; Russian Orthodox, 2.5%; Protestant, 1.3%; other (mostly nonreligious), 24.0%.

Major cities (1996): Vilnius, 573,200; Kaunas, 410,800; Klaipeda, 201,500; Siauliai, 146,500; Panevežys, 132,300; Alytus, 77,400.

Vital Statistics

Birth rate per 1,000 population (1996): 10.6; (1995) legitimate, 87.4%; illegitimate, 12.6%.

Death rate per 1,000 population (1996): 11.6.

Natural increase rate per 1,000 population (1996): –1.0.

Total fertility rate (avg. births per childbearing woman; 1995): 1.5.

Marriage rate per 1,000 population (1995): 6.0.

Divorce rate per 1,000 population (1995): 2.8.

Life expectancy at birth (1995): male, 63.6 years; female, 75.2 years.

Major causes of death per 100,000 population (1995): circulatory diseases, 654; cancers, 203; accidents, 176; respiratory diseases, 49; digestive diseases, 32.

National Economy

Production (metric tons except as noted):

Agriculture, forestry, fishing (1996): potatoes, 1,594,000; barley, 1,000,000; wheat, 550,000; sugar beets, 650,000; livestock (number of live animals) 1,150,000 pigs; 1,100,000 cattle; 8,530,000 poultry; roundwood, (1995) 4,495,000 cu. m.; fish catch (1993), 120,078.

Mining and quarrying (1995): limestone 3,000,000; peat 214,000.

Manufacturing (value of production in '000 litai; 1995): processed foods, 4,781,421; textile and knitwear, 1,748,812; chemicals, 1,066,200; wood and wood products, 630,334.

Household income and expenditure (1995):

Average household size (1989), 3.2.

Sources of income: wages, 71.4%; pensions and grants, 14.0%; self-employment in agriculture, 6.6%; other, 7.0%.

Expenditure: food, 45.1%; nonfood goods, 17.6%; services, 15.6%; taxes, 14.4%; agricultural expenses, 4.3%.

Gross national product (1996): US$8,455,000,000 (US$2,280 per capita).

Tourism (1995): receipts from visitors, US$124,000,000; expenditures by nationals abroad, US$138,000,000.

Land use (1994): forested, 30.4%; meadows and pastures, 7.6%; agricultural and under permanent cultivation, 53.9%; other, 8.1%.

Foreign Trade

Imports (1995): petroleum and gas, 26.7%; machinery, 16.5%; textiles, 9.3%; chemicals, 9.0%; transport equipment, 7.5%; base metals, 6.7%; prepared foods, 4.5%.

Major import sources: Russia, 31.1%; Germany, 15.2%; United Kingdom, 4.3%; Poland, 4.1%; Denmark, 3.9%; Finland, 3.6%.

Exports (1995): textiles, 14.7%; chemicals, 12.2%; mineral products, 11.9%; machinery, 10.8%; base metals, 8.7%; live animals, 8.4%; prepared foods, 5.6%.

Major export destinations: Russia, 20.4%; Germany, 14.4%; Belarus, 10.7%; Ukraine, 7.5%; Latvia, 7.1%; The Netherlands, 4.9%; Poland, 3.9%.

Transport

Railroads (1995): length, 1,802 mi. (2,900 km.); passenger-mi., 702,000,000 (passenger-km., 1,130,000,000); short ton-mi. cargo, 5,264,000,000 (metric ton-km. cargo, 7,685,000,000).

Roads (1995): total length, 38,178 mi. (61,442 km.); paved, 86%.

Vehicles (1995): passenger cars, 718,469; trucks and buses, 110,696.

Merchant marine (1995): vessels (100 gross tons and over), 95; total deadweight tonnage, 569,288.

Air transport (1996): passenger-mi., 226,000,000 (passenger-km., 363,000,000); short ton-mi. cargo, 1,566,000 (metric ton-km. cargo, 2,287,000); airports with scheduled flights (1996), 3.

Education and Health

Educational attainment (1989): percentage of population age 25 and over having no schooling, 9.1%; complete primary education, 21.3%; incomplete secondary, 57.0%; higher, 12.6%.

Literacy (1995): total population age 15 and over literate, 99.5%; males literate, 99.6%; females literate, 99.3%.

Health (1995): physicians, 14,737 (1 per 252 persons); hospital beds, 40,262 (1 per 92 persons); infant mortality rate per 1,000 live births, 12.4.

Military

Total active duty personnel (1996): 5,100 (army, 82.3%; navy, 6.9%; air force, 10.8%).

Military expenditure as percentage of GNP (1995): 0.5%, (world, 2.8%); per capita expenditure, US$21.

NOTES

INTRODUCTION: SIMILAR BUT DISTINCT

1. Quoted in Walter R. Iwaskiw, ed., *Estonia, Latvia, and Lithuania Country Studies.* Lanham, MD: Library of Congress, 1996, p. xix.
2. Quoted in the Baltics Worldwide, www.balticsww.com/ tourist/index.html.
3. Quoted in the Baltics Worldwide, www.balticsww.com/ tourist/estonia/index.htm.
4. Quoted in the Baltics Worldwide, www.balticsww.com/ quotes/latquotes.htm.

CHAPTER 1: A LONG, EMBATTLED HISTORY

5. Quoted in Roger Williams, ed., *Baltic States.* London: APA Publications, 1996, p. 132.
6. Quoted in the Baltics Worldwide, www.balticsww.com/ timeline.htm.

CHAPTER 2: THE ROAD TO INDEPENDENCE

7. Quoted in Williams, *Baltic States,* p. 136.
8. Quoted in the Baltics Worldwide, www.balticsww.com/ timeline.htm.
9. Quoted in "The Baltics Set the Agenda," *Time,* August 28, 1989, p. 27.
10. Quoted in Priit J. Vesilind, "The Baltic Nations," *National Geographic,* November 1990, p. 14.
11. Quoted in the Baltics Worldwide, www.balticsww.com/ timeline.htm.

CHAPTER 3: AN INTERMINGLING OF CULTURES

12. Quoted in the Baltics Worldwide, www.balticsww.com/ quotes/estquotes.htm.

13. Quoted in Vesilind, "The Baltic Nations," p. 35.

14. Quoted in Soros Foundations Network, www.soros.org/ fmp2/html/baltics.htm.

CHAPTER 4: A TRADITION BASED IN FOLKLORE AND NATIONAL PRIDE

15. Quoted in Williams, *Baltic States*, p. 82.

16. Quoted in Litnet, www.litnet/lt/ciurlionis/ciurlion.html.

CHAPTER 5: FACING THE NEW MILLENNIUM

17. Quoted in the Baltics Worldwide, www.balticsww.com/ quotes/busiquotes.htm.

18. Quoted in the Baltics Worldwide, www.balticsww.com/ quotes/economy.htm.

19. Quoted in Williams, *Baltic States*, p. 113.

CHRONOLOGY

B.C.

3000
Ancestors of modern Estonians, Latvians, and Lithuanians establish themselves along the Baltic coast.

A.D.

650
Viking raids begin years of trading between the Scandinavians and Baltic tribes.

1180
Meinhard of Bremen lands on the coast of present-day Latvia to preach Christianity to Livs.

1201
Riga is founded by German crusaders under Albrecht of Bremen.

1219
Danes take Tallinn.

1230
Lithuanian tribes unite under Mindaugas.

1236
Lithuanians defeat Livonian knights in the battle of Saule.

1237
German crusaders' Order of the Knights of the Sword becomes the Teutonic Order.

1253
Mindaugas adopts Christianity and is crowned king of Lithuania.

1282
Riga joins the Hanseatic League.

1285
Tallinn joins the Hanseatic League.

1316
Lithuanian expansion begins under Duke Gediminas.

1343
Estonian rebellion on St. George's Night leads to Danes selling duchy of Estonia to the Teutonic Order.

1386
Lithuania and Poland unite as a result of the marriage between Duke Jogaila and Queen Jadwiga.

1410
Teutonic Knights are defeated at Tannenberg by Duke Vytautas and Jogaila.

1520s
Reformation establishes Lutheranism in Latvia and Estonia.

1558–1583
The Livonian War between Sweden and Russia results in the division of Livonia.

1569
Poland and Lithuania are formally united.

1579
Vilnius University is founded by Jesuits.

1600–1629
The Polish-Swedish War divides the Baltics between Poland and Sweden.

1632
Tartu University in Estonia is founded.

1700–1721
The Great Northern War between Charles XII of Sweden and Peter the Great results in Russian victory; Russia occupies Estonia and Latvia.

1795
Lithuania follows Latvia and Estonia into the Russian Empire.

1811
Serfs in Estonia are emancipated.

1830
A Lithuanian-Polish uprising against Russia occurs.

1854
The Estonian national epic *Kalevipoeg* is published.

1860–1885
The National Awakening.

1869
The first national singing festival is held in Tartu.

1870
The railway between Tallinn and St. Petersburg is completed.

1885
The era of intense Russification begins.

1888
The Latvian national epic *Lacplesis* is published.

1905
A general strike in the Baltic States accompanies upheavals in the Russian Empire.

1914
World War I begins.

1915
Lithuania is occupied by German troops.

1917
Revolutions occur in Russia; Communists seize power.

1918
Lithuania declares its independence, followed by Estonia and Latvia.

1920
The Baltic States sign peace treaties with Soviet Russia; independence is achieved for the first time in Estonia and Latvia, and for the first time since the grand duchy in Lithuania; Poland seizes Vilnius.

1920–1922
Democratic constitutions are introduced.

1921
Estonia, Latvia, and Lithuania are admitted to the League of Nations.

1922
The Soviet Union is formed.

1934
Lithuania joins Estonia and Latvia to form the Baltic Entente.

1939
The Molotov-Ribbentrop Pact puts the Baltic States in the Soviet sphere of influence.

1940–1941

The Russian army occupies the Baltics; states are absorbed into the Soviet Union; thousands are deported or shot.

1941–1944
Germany occupies the Baltics; hundreds of thousands of Jews are killed.

1944
The Russian army once again returns to the Baltics; the Stalinist era begins; more people are deported to Siberia.

1952
Guerrilla resistance to the Soviet Union ends in the Baltics.

1953
Soviet repression eases after the death of Stalin.

1972
Students and workers protest against Soviet rule; Romas Kalanta immolates himself; *The Chronicle of the Lithuanian Catholic Church* begins publication.

1978
August Sabe, the last Forest Brother, dies.

1985
Mikhail Gorbachev comes to power in the USSR, introducing the policies of glasnost and perestroika.

1986–1987
Demonstrations are held to protest the environmental destruction by Soviet industry and armed forces.

1988
The Popular Fronts in Estonia, Latvia, and Lithuania are founded.

1989

A 430-mile-long human chain stretches across the Baltics to commemorate the fiftieth anniversary of the Molotov-Ribbentrop Pact; the Lithuanian Communist Party separates from the Soviet Party.

1990

Lithuania, Latvia, and Estonia vote to restore independence.

1991

Gorbachev survives an attempted coup; Soviet intervention results in fourteen deaths in Lithuania, and five in Latvia; the USSR recognizes Lithuanian, Latvian, and Estonian independence; the Soviet Union is dissolved; the Commonwealth of Independent States is formed.

1994

Russian troops pull out of the Baltics; the *MS Estonia* sinks.

1999

Vaira Vike-Freiberga is sworn in as president of Latvia, the first female head of state in Eastern Europe.

GLOSSARY

amber: Petrified resin from pine trees.

crusader: A Christian soldier who waged wars of conquest in the eleventh, twelfth, or thirteenth centuries.

daina: A Latvian folk song consisting of a poem sung to an ancient melody.

glasnost: The Soviet policy of openness that eased restrictions on writing and speech.

kroon: The Estonian unit of currency.

lat: The Latvian unit of currency.

litas: The Lithuanian unit of currency.

perestroika: The restructuring of Soviet society.

phosphorite: Rock containing phosphates, used in the production of fertilizers.

Riigikogu: The Estonian legislature.

Saeima: The Latvian legislature.

Seimas: The Lithuanian legislature.

Suggestions for Further Reading

Books

Fred Coleman, *The Decline and Fall of the Soviet Empire.* New York: St. Martin's Press, 1996. This book is a detailed history of the Soviet Union from the period after Stalin's death through 1991.

Ronald Hingley, *Russia: A Concise History.* New York: Thames and Hudson, 1991. This history of the Soviet Union, from its start as a small Slavic community to its status as a superpower, contains many pictures and illustrations.

Michael G. Kort, *The Handbook of the Former Soviet Union.* Brookfield, CT: Millbrook Press, 1997. Kort's book focuses on the development of the nations formed from the former Soviet Union. Nearly half the book consists of an encyclopedic listing of important cities, public figures, ethnic groups, and important issues facing these nations.

Mart Laar, *War in the Woods: Estonia's Struggle for Survival 1944–1956.* Trans. Tiina Ets. Washington, DC: Compass Press, 1992. This detailed work examines the history of the Baltic nationalist resistance movement, focusing on the Forest Brothers.

John R. Matthews, *The Rise and Fall of the Soviet Union.* San Diego, CA: Lucent Books, 2000. This book in the World History Series traces the history of the Soviet Union from 1917 through 1991.

Paul A. Winters, ed., *The Collapse of the Soviet Union.* San Diego, CA: Greenhaven Press, 1999. This volume in the Turning Points in World History Series examines the collapse of the Soviet Union through twenty-one essays.

Periodicals

George Church, "Anatomy of a Coup," *Time*, September 2, 1991.

———, "The End of the U.S.S.R.," *Time*, December 23, 1991.

John Kohan, "Cry Independence," *Time*, August 21, 1989.

James Walsh, "The Iron Fist," *Time*, January 21, 1991.

WORKS CONSULTED

BOOKS

Stephen Baister and Chris Patrick, *Latvia: The Bradt Travel Guide*. Bucks, England: Bradt Publications, 1999. This volume in the Bradt Travel Guide Series examines topics of interest to those who'd like to visit this Baltic nation.

Walter R. Iwaskiw, ed., *Estonia, Latvia, and Lithuania Country Studies*. Lanham, MD: Library of Congress, 1996. This volume in the Library of Congress Area Handbook Series gives a detailed look at the political, economic, and social institutions of the Baltic nations.

Gordon McLachlan, *Lithuania: The Bradt Travel Guide*. Bucks, England: Bradt Publications, 1999. Another volume in the Bradt Travel Guide Series.

M. Wesley Shoemaker, *Russia, Eurasian States, and Eastern Europe 1996*. Harpers Ferry, W V: Stryker-Post Publications, 1996. This volume in the World Today Series thoroughly examines each of the nations of Eastern Europe and the republics that composed the former Soviet Union.

Neil Taylor, *Estonia: The Bradt Travel Guide*. Bucks, England: Bradt Publications, 1999. Another volume in the Bradt Travel Guide Series.

Roger Williams, ed., *Baltic States*. London: APA Publications, 1996. This volume in the Insight Guides Series gives a detailed look at the Baltic region, with an excellent section on the history of Estonia, Latvia, and Lithuania.

PERIODICALS

"The Baltics Set the Agenda," *Time*, August 28, 1989.

Priit J. Vesilind, "The Baltic Nations," *National Geographic*, November 1990.

WEBSITES

The Baltics Worldwide (www.balticsww.com). Website produced by the pan-Baltic magazine *City Paper: The Baltic States.*

Britannica.Com (www.britannica.com). Website of the *Encyclopaedia Britannica.*

Catholic Shrines (www.catholicshrines.com). Website on Catholic shrines throughout Europe.

Litnet (www.litnet.lt). Website for the Academical and Research Network in Lithuania.

Soros Foundations Network (www.soros.org). Website of the foundation dedicated to building open societies around the world.

INDEX

PICTURE CREDITS

ABOUT THE AUTHOR

John F. Grabowski is a native of Brooklyn, New York. He holds a bachelor's degree in psychology from City College of New York and a master's degree in educational psychology from Teacher's College, Columbia University. He has been a teacher for thirty-one years, as well as a freelance writer, specializing in the fields of sports, education, and comedy. His body of published work includes twenty-four books; a nationally syndicated sports column; consultation on several math textbooks; articles for newspapers, magazines, and the programs of professional sports teams; and comedy material sold to Jay Leno, Joan Rivers, and numerous other comics. He and his wife, Patricia, live in Staten Island with their daughter, Elizabeth.